*The power to forgive is within your reach.
You can do it.*

While every precaution has been taken in the preparation of this book, the publisher assumes no responsibility for errors or omissions, or for damages resulting from the use of the information contained herein.

GIRL, FORGIVE THEM AND MOVE ON

First edition. July 4, 2024.

Copyright © 2024 Kim Ruff-Moore.

ISBN: 979-8224827916

Written by Kim Ruff-Moore.

Girl, Forgive Them And Move On

By Kim Ruff- Moore

Other Titles Available by Kim Ruff Moore:
Books for Adults:

"Never Put All Your Eggs in One Basket"
"Serendipity"
"Cuffed"
"Marriage Releases God's Favor"
"Superheroes Teach"
"I Speak Life"
"I Speak Life Devotional"
"Secrets of a Successful Published Author"
"Jealousy Makes You Sick"
"Waymaker"
"Girl, Mash The Gas: Stop Procrastinating

CHILDREN'S BOOKS:

Suzzie Mocha Series
Pavo the Parrot
Otis the Brown Bear
Kirby the Koala Series
The Land of Unicorns Series
Spence Seven Series
Harper Sharper Series
Sergio The Studio Mouse Series
Rosie and the Easter Egg Hunt

Table of Contents

Introduction

In our journey through life, we've all encountered moments of betrayal or wrongdoing, whether by someone close to us or a stranger. These memories linger, etched into the fabric of our existence. The pain runs deep, leaving scars that sometimes seem impossible to heal. Yet, despite the hurt inflicted upon us, we are faced with a choice: to cling onto resentment and bitterness, or to find the courage to forgive.

Forgiveness is a formidable force, capable of liberating us from the shackles of anger and hurt. It's not about condoning the wrongs done to us; rather, it's about releasing ourselves from the burden of carrying that pain. Harboring unforgiveness is like building a prison within our hearts, trapping us in a cycle of negativity and despair. Meanwhile, the offender may remain oblivious to the havoc they've caused, or worse, indifferent to our suffering.

But forgiveness isn't just about setting ourselves free; it's also a divine mandate. As the Bible teaches, "For all have sinned and fall short of the glory of God." By extending forgiveness to others, we open the door for our own redemption. It's a profound act of humility and grace, echoing the mercy that our Heavenly Father extends to us.

In the pages of this book, we'll delve deep into the essence of forgiveness—the power it holds to transform lives, heal wounds, and restore relationships. Through personal anecdotes, timeless wisdom, and practical insights, we'll explore the journey towards forgiveness and the profound impact it can have on our spiritual and emotional well-being. Whether you're grappling with past hurts or seeking to cultivate a spirit of forgiveness in your daily life, this book is a roadmap to embracing the liberating power of forgiveness and experiencing the freedom it brings.

WITHIN THESE PAGES, we'll navigate the complexities of forgiveness with honesty and compassion. We'll confront the raw emotions that accompany betrayal and wrongdoing, acknowledging the depth of pain they inflict. Through shared experiences and reflective exercises, we'll uncover the roots of resentment and bitterness, unraveling the tangled threads of hurt that bind us.

But our journey won't end there. We'll journey together towards a place of healing and wholeness, discovering the transformative power of forgiveness. Along the way, we'll learn to let go of the need for retribution and embrace empathy instead, recognizing the humanity in both ourselves and those who have wronged us. Through forgiveness, we'll break free from the chains of the past and step into a future filled with hope and possibility.

Forgiveness is not a one-time event but a continual process—a journey of the heart that requires patience, perseverance, and faith. As we embark on this journey together, may we find solace in the knowledge that we are not alone. With each step we take towards forgiveness, we draw closer to the divine love that sustains us and the peace that surpasses all understanding.

So let us embark on this transformative journey together, as we explore the depths of forgiveness and unlock the boundless potential it holds for our lives. Through the power of forgiveness, may we find healing, redemption, and ultimately, freedom.

As we continue our exploration of forgiveness, we'll delve into practical strategies for navigating the complexities of letting go and moving forward. We'll uncover the importance of self-forgiveness, recognizing that healing begins within ourselves. Through self-reflection and self-compassion, we'll learn to release the guilt and shame that often accompany our own mistakes and shortcomings.

Moreover, we'll explore the dynamics of forgiveness in various relationships, whether it's repairing fractured bonds with family members, friends, or even colleagues. We'll examine the role of communication, empathy, and boundaries in the process of reconciliation, understanding that forgiveness does not always mean reconciliation but can instead pave the way for healthy detachment and closure.

Throughout our journey, we'll draw inspiration from the stories of resilience and redemption, discovering how forgiveness has the power to turn pain into purpose and wounds into wisdom. We'll reflect on the lives of forgiveness champions who have exemplified grace in the face of adversity, showing us that even in the darkest of times, forgiveness is a beacon of light.

Ultimately, this book is a testament to the transformative power of forgiveness—a power that transcends boundaries of culture, religion, and time. It is my hope that through these words, you will find the courage to embark on your own journey of forgiveness, knowing that in doing so, you are reclaiming your power, your peace, and your freedom.

In examining my decision to forgive, I found myself embarking on a profound journey of introspection and spiritual growth. My life's narrative has been punctuated by moments of betrayal and hurt, inflicted by those closest to me as well as strangers who crossed my path. At times, the weight of these grievances seemed insurmountable, leaving me grappling with feelings of anger, resentment, and confusion. Yet, amid the darkness, I turned to the guiding light of faith, seeking solace and understanding in the teachings of the Bible.

As I immersed myself in prayer and reflection, I felt a stirring within my soul—a gentle nudge from the divine urging me to confront the pain and bitterness that had taken root within me. It was a daunting task, requiring a deep level of honesty and vulnerability. But with each whispered prayer, I felt my heart gradually softening, surrendering to the transformative power of divine grace.

Through prayer and introspection, I began to see forgiveness not as a sign of weakness, but as an act of courage and obedience to God's commandments. I realized that holding onto grudges only served to imprison me in a cycle of negativity and despair, hindering my spiritual growth and emotional well-being. It was only by relinquishing my grip on past hurts and grievances that I could experience true freedom and healing.

In surrendering to God's will, I found the strength to forgive those who had wronged me—not because they deserved it, but because I deserved peace. It was a humbling realization, one that required me to extend the same grace and mercy that had been bestowed upon me by a loving and forgiving God. And as I embraced forgiveness, I felt a profound sense of liberation—a weight lifted from my shoulders, replaced by a deep and abiding sense of peace.

The decision to forgive taught me that forgiveness is not just a moral obligation, but a spiritual imperative—a sacred duty that opens the door to healing, reconciliation, and divine grace. It is my prayer that others may find the same solace and redemption in the transformative power of forgiveness, and that through God's unfailing love, all wounds may be healed, and all hearts may be set free.

AS I CONTINUED TO NAVIGATE the path of forgiveness, I encountered moments of resistance and doubt. There were times when the wounds felt too raw, the pain too deep to let go. Yet, in those moments of struggle, I turned to the teachings of the Bible for guidance and reassurance.

I found solace in the words of Jesus, who exemplified forgiveness even in the face of unimaginable suffering. His profound act of forgiveness on the cross, extending mercy to those who crucified Him, served as a powerful reminder of the boundless love and grace of God. If He could forgive in the midst of such agony, then surely I too could find the strength to forgive.

With each step forward, I felt the burden of resentment and bitterness gradually lifting from my shoulders. I learned to release the need for justice or retribution, trusting instead in God's divine plan for redemption and restoration. And as I surrendered my pain to Him, I discovered a newfound sense of peace and wholeness.

Through prayer and reflection, I came to understand that forgiveness is not a one-time event, but a daily practice—a continual surrendering of my heart to God's will. It requires humility, patience, and an unwavering faith in His promises. Yet, in the midst of the struggle, I found beauty in the journey—a journey that led me closer to God and to the true essence of forgiveness.

As I look back on my journey, I am filled with gratitude for the healing and transformation that forgiveness has brought into my life. It has allowed me to release the chains of the past and embrace a future filled with hope and possibility. And though the road ahead may be fraught with challenges, I walk forward with confidence, knowing that God's love and grace will guide me every step of the way.

In continuing to embrace forgiveness, I've come to realize its profound impact not only on my own life but also on my relationships with others. As I extend grace and mercy to those who have wronged me, I've witnessed walls of resentment crumble, replaced by bridges of understanding and reconciliation.

Forgiveness has the power to mend broken relationships, to bridge the chasm of misunderstanding, and to foster a sense of empathy and compassion for others. Through forgiveness, I've learned to see beyond the faults and shortcomings of those around me, recognizing the inherent dignity and worth in every individual.

Moreover, I've come to understand that forgiveness is not just about absolving others of their wrongs, but also about setting myself free from the bondage of anger and bitterness. By releasing the grip of past hurts, I've opened myself up to a life filled with joy, peace, and love.

In the words of the psalmist, "Search me, God, and know my heart; test me and know my anxious thoughts. See if there is any offensive way in me, and lead me in the way everlasting" (Psalm 139:23-24, NIV). Through prayer and introspection, I've invited God to examine my heart, to reveal any lingering resentment or unforgiveness, and to guide me on the path of righteousness.

As I continue to walk this journey of forgiveness, I am reminded of the words of Jesus, who taught us to pray, "Forgive us our sins, as we forgive those who sin against us" (Matthew 6:12, NLT). In extending forgiveness to others, I am reminded of the immeasurable grace and mercy that God has bestowed upon me, and I am humbled by the opportunity to reflect His love in my own life.

True forgiveness has been a transformative journey—one that has challenged me to confront my deepest hurts and to embrace the liberating power of forgiveness. Through prayer, reflection, and unwavering faith, I have discovered a newfound sense of peace, purpose, and joy. And as I continue to walk in the footsteps of Jesus, I am confident that His love will guide me every step of the way.

The Power of Forgiveness

Reflecting on some of the darker moments of my life, one particular event stands out vividly—a time when I found myself targeted by a group of women at work who seemed determined to undermine me at every turn. It was a new job for me, and I was still finding my footing, lacking the experience and confidence to defend myself against their relentless campaign of sabotage.

These women went to great lengths to tarnish my reputation, spreading rumors and lies to make me appear incompetent. They even went so far as to tamper with the data I had entered into the computer, all in an effort to discredit me and undermine my work. It was a difficult and demoralizing experience, one that left me feeling betrayed and utterly alone.

But in the midst of the darkness, I made a choice—a choice to forgive. It wasn't easy, and it certainly didn't happen overnight, but I knew that harboring resentment and bitterness would only poison my own heart. So, I turned to God, seeking His guidance and strength to help me let go of the pain and anger that consumed me.

Through prayer and reflection, I began to see forgiveness not as a sign of weakness, but as a source of empowerment. By choosing to forgive, I was taking back control of my own life, refusing to let the actions of others define me or dictate my happiness. It was a liberating realization—one that filled me with a sense of peace and freedom I hadn't felt in a long time.

Forgiving those women wasn't about excusing their behavior or pretending that the hurt they caused didn't matter. It was about acknowledging the pain, releasing it, and choosing to move forward with grace and dignity. And in doing so, I discovered a strength within myself that I never knew existed—a strength born out of resilience, faith, and the unwavering belief that love and forgiveness have the power to conquer even the darkest of days.

Today, as I look back on that challenging chapter of my life, I am filled with gratitude for the lessons it taught me. I am grateful for the opportunity to experience the transformative power of forgiveness—to witness firsthand how it can heal wounds, mend broken hearts, and set the soul free. And though the scars of that experience may still linger, they serve as a reminder of my own resilience and the boundless grace of a loving God who never abandoned me, even in my darkest hour.

In the aftermath of that challenging experience, forgiveness became a beacon of light guiding me through the darkness. It wasn't a one-time decision, but rather a daily practice—a conscious effort to let go of the hurt and anger that threatened to consume me. Each day brought new opportunities to extend grace and mercy to those who had wronged me, even when the wounds still felt raw and the pain seemed insurmountable.

As I continued to lean on my faith and seek solace in prayer, I discovered the power of forgiveness to transform not only my own heart but also my perspective on life. Instead of dwelling on the injustices I had faced, I began to focus on the blessings that surrounded me—the love of family and friends, the beauty of nature, and the infinite possibilities that lay ahead.

Through forgiveness, I found the strength to rise above the negativity and reclaim my sense of worth and dignity. I refused to allow the actions of others to define my value or dictate my future. Instead, I embraced my own inherent worth as a child of God, worthy of love and respect regardless of the opinions of others.

Moreover, forgiveness opened the door to healing and reconciliation in unexpected ways. While I may never forget the pain inflicted upon me, I found it within myself to extend an olive branch to those who had wronged me, offering them the opportunity to make amends and move forward together in peace.

In the end, forgiveness was not just about letting go of the past, but also about embracing the possibilities of the future. It was about reclaiming my power and choosing to live a life filled with love, joy, and purpose. And as I continue on this journey of forgiveness, I am grateful for the strength and resilience it has instilled within me, guiding me towards a brighter tomorrow filled with hope and possibility.

In the midst of navigating the turmoil at work, there was another layer of hurt and frustration that I had to confront—the realization that even those in positions of authority, who were supposed to protect and support their employees, failed to intervene. I found myself grappling with feelings of betrayal and disappointment as I watched the one in charge turn a blind eye to the injustices being perpetrated against me.

It was a bitter pill to swallow, realizing that politics and small-town agendas took precedence over fairness and integrity. Despite my pleas for help and intervention, I was met with indifference and silence. It felt like a slap in the face, adding insult to injury and deepening the wounds that had already been inflicted upon me.

In those moments of despair, I was tempted to succumb to bitterness and resentment, to lash out in anger at those who had failed me. But as I reflected on the teachings of forgiveness, I knew that holding onto grudges would only poison my own heart. So, I made the conscious decision to extend forgiveness even to those who had failed me—the ones who had turned their backs when I needed them the most.

It wasn't easy, by any means. There were days when the pain felt overwhelming, when I struggled to find the strength to forgive. But through prayer and perseverance, I found the courage to release the anger and hurt that threatened to consume me. I chose to entrust justice to a higher power, believing that ultimately, truth would prevail and justice would be served.

In forgiving those who had failed me, I reclaimed my power and refused to be defined by the actions of others. I chose to focus on the lessons learned and the growth that had come from adversity, rather than dwelling on the injustices of the past. And in doing so, I found a sense of peace and liberation that transcended the pain and frustration of the situation.

Looking back, I am grateful for the opportunity to experience the transformative power of forgiveness in the face of adversity. It taught me that true strength lies not in holding onto grudges, but in letting go and embracing the healing power of

love and compassion. And though the scars of that experience may still linger, they serve as a reminder of my own resilience and the boundless grace of a loving God who never abandoned me, even in my darkest hour.

Finding the faith and resolve to forgive amidst the turmoil was a truly refreshing experience—a moment of clarity and liberation that transcended the pain and frustration of the situation. It was a decision born out of necessity, driven by the understanding that holding onto bitterness and resentment would only serve to poison my own heart. So, I chose to embrace forgiveness as an act of self-preservation, as a means of reclaiming my power and refusing to be defined by the actions of others.

The outcome of the turmoil at work was nothing short of disheartening. Not only was I portrayed as incompetent, but I was also removed from the job I had worked so hard for, thrust into a position that I had never applied for and that nobody seemed to want. It felt like a slap in the face—a cruel twist of fate that left me questioning my worth and my place in the world. But even in the midst of adversity, I held onto the belief that God had a plan for me—a plan that far exceeded the narrow confines of my current circumstances.

As I settled into my new role, I found myself grappling with feelings of resentment and frustration. It was difficult not to dwell on the injustices that had been inflicted upon me, to resist the temptation to harbor ill will towards those who had wronged me. But as I reflected on the teachings of forgiveness, I realized that holding onto anger would only serve to perpetuate the cycle of negativity and despair. So, I made the conscious choice to extend forgiveness to those who had hurt me—to release the burden of bitterness and resentment and embrace a future filled with hope and possibility.

In the years that followed, I discovered that God had indeed turned lemons into lemonade. Despite the challenges I faced, I found fulfillment and purpose in my new role, making a difference in the lives of those around me. I poured my heart and soul into my work, determined to prove that my worth was not defined by the opinions of others. And as I embraced forgiveness and let go of the past, I found a sense of peace and contentment that transcended the trials and tribulations of my journey.

Looking back, I am grateful for the opportunity to experience the transformative power of forgiveness in the face of adversity. It taught me that even in the darkest of times, there is always light to be found—that by choosing love over hate, grace over judgment, we can overcome even the most daunting of obstacles. And though the scars of that experience may still linger, they serve as a testament to my strength, resilience, and unwavering faith in a God who can turn even the most dire of circumstances into something beautiful.

Forgiving those who had orchestrated my downfall wasn't just about letting go of past grievances; it was about reclaiming my own sense of worth and dignity. It was a declaration that their actions would not define me, that I would rise above the injustice and prove my worth through my actions and character. And as I immersed myself in my new role, I discovered a sense of purpose and fulfillment that I hadn't known before.

Despite the initial challenges and setbacks, I persevered, determined to make the most of the opportunity that had been presented to me. I poured my energy into my work, striving to excel in every task and make a positive impact in my new environment. And as time went on, I began to see the fruits of my labor—the relationships I built, the accomplishments I achieved, and the lives I touched along the way.

In hindsight, I realized that being removed from that toxic environment was a blessing in disguise. It allowed me to break free from the chains of negativity and toxicity, to step into a new chapter of my life filled with hope and possibility. And though the journey was not without its challenges, I emerged stronger, wiser, and more resilient than ever before.

As I reflect on those turbulent times, I am reminded of the words of Jesus, who taught us to love our enemies and pray for those who persecute us. In extending forgiveness to those who had wronged me, I found a sense of peace and freedom that transcended the pain and bitterness of the past. It was a testament to the transformative power of forgiveness—a power that has the ability to heal wounds, mend broken hearts, and set the soul free.

Today, I stand as a living testimony to the power of forgiveness—a testament to the fact that even in the darkest of times, there is always hope for redemption and renewal. And though the journey may be long and arduous, I am grateful for the opportunity to experience the transformative power of forgiveness firsthand. It has taught me that by choosing love over hate, grace over judgment, we can overcome even the most daunting of obstacles and emerge stronger, wiser, and more compassionate than ever before.

Freedom In Letting It Go

Learning to let go of unforgiveness toward people who've harmed or betrayed me has been a journey of empowerment, lifting a tremendous weight off not just my shoulders, but also my spirit. It's challenging to ask for God's forgiveness when harboring feelings of resentment toward others for their actions. My own journey of letting go became a crucial part of what I believe God was preparing to do in my life. Throughout my lifetime, I've encountered numerous individuals who've opposed me—overachievers, the attractive, the talented, the successful—will always have haters. Yet, finding the freedom in letting go was transformative. It's like shedding layers of bitterness and negativity, making space for growth and positivity. This process wasn't easy; it required introspection, humility, and a willingness to release the grip of hurt and anger. But with every step toward forgiveness, I felt lighter, more liberated, and more aligned with the grace and love that I believe God extends to us all. In the end, letting go of unforgiveness wasn't just about those who wronged me—it was about reclaiming my own peace and moving forward with a heart unburdened by the weight of resentment.

As I reflected deeper into the process of forgiveness, I realized that holding onto grudges only perpetuates a cycle of pain and negativity. It's like carrying around a heavy backpack filled with stones; the longer you bear it, the more it weighs you down. By choosing to let go, I unburdened myself from this unnecessary load, allowing myself to walk more freely and lightly through life.

Also, I came to understand that forgiveness doesn't mean excusing or condoning the actions of others. Instead, it's a conscious decision to release the hold those actions have on your heart and mind. It's about acknowledging the hurt, processing it, and then choosing to move forward without letting it define you.

In my own journey, I found solace in prayer and reflection. I sought guidance from spiritual teachings and leaned on my faith to find the strength to forgive. And as I let go of past grievances, I felt a profound sense of liberation and inner peace wash over me.

But perhaps the most remarkable aspect of forgiveness is its ripple effect. As I forgave others, I also found it easier to forgive myself for past mistakes and shortcomings. This self-compassion opened the door to deeper healing and self-growth, enabling me to embrace my humanity with greater humility and grace.

Ultimately, letting go of unforgiveness has been a transformative experience—one that has enriched my spiritual journey and liberated me from the shackles of resentment. It's taught me that true strength lies not in holding onto anger, but in having the courage to forgive and embrace the freedom that comes with it.

In continuing my journey of forgiveness, I've learned that it's not a one-time event but rather an ongoing process. There are moments when old wounds resurface, triggering feelings of resentment or anger. In those moments, I remind myself of the peace and liberation I've found through forgiveness, and I consciously choose to let go once again.

Moreover, I've come to recognize that forgiveness is a gift—to both myself and to those I forgive. It's a gift of freedom from the past, allowing me to live more fully in the present and to approach the future with hope and optimism. And it's a gift of grace, extending to others the same mercy and compassion that I hope to receive myself.

Through forgiveness, I've also discovered the power of empathy and understanding. By seeking to understand the motivations and struggles of those who have wronged me, I've been able to see them not as enemies, but as fellow human beings in need of love and healing. This shift in perspective has deepened my capacity for compassion and empathy, fostering greater harmony and connection in my relationships.

Basically, my journey of forgiveness has been both challenging and rewarding. It has required courage, humility, and a willingness to let go of pride and ego. But the rewards have been immeasurable—a heart filled with peace, a spirit lifted by grace, and a newfound sense of freedom to live and love more fully. And for that, I am deeply grateful.

I remember the day vividly, the day I made the conscious decision to let go of the weight of unforgiveness that had been burdening my heart for far too long. I found myself kneeling in prayer, petitioning Christ for guidance and strength. In that moment, I realized that forgiveness was not just a choice, but a necessary step on my spiritual journey. If I wanted to walk the path of love and grace, if I wanted to see Jesus one day, I knew I had to release the bitterness and resentment I harbored toward those who had wronged me.

As I poured out my heart to God, I laid bare the names of those who had caused me pain—the ones who opposed me, who betrayed my trust, who sought to harm me and my family. I cried out for help in forgiving them, knowing full well that it was a tall order. The sting of their actions lingered, haunting me whenever I saw their faces or heard their names. Yet, in that moment of surrender, something shifted within me.

Forgiveness didn't mean forgetting or excusing what had been done to me. It wasn't about letting the offenders off the hook or pretending that the hurt never happened. Instead, it was about releasing the hold that their actions had over me, refusing to let their negativity define my life any longer.

In a way, forgiveness was like a lesson learned the hard way, akin to a child touching a hot stove and getting burned. The pain serves as a reminder to approach with caution in the future, but it doesn't mean avoiding the stove altogether. Just as the stove is necessary for cooking, so too are the challenges and conflicts we face in life. They shape us, teach us, and ultimately strengthen us—if we allow them to.

So, while I may never forget the pain inflicted upon me, I choose to let go of the bitterness and resentment that once consumed me. In doing so, I reclaim my power, my peace, and my ability to live with an open heart. And though the journey of forgiveness may be long and arduous, the freedom it brings is worth every step.

I ultimately found that it wasn't a one-time event, but rather a daily practice—a conscious choice I had to make anew each day. There were moments when old wounds resurfaced, triggering familiar feelings of anger or hurt. In those moments, I had to remind myself of the commitment I made to release the past and embrace a future filled with love and grace..

With time, I came to understand that forgiveness was as much a gift to myself as it was to others. By letting go of resentment and anger, I freed myself from the emotional shackles that had bound me for so long. I experienced a newfound sense of inner peace and liberation—a weightlessness that allowed me to soar above the petty grievances of the past and embrace the fullness of life in the present moment.

But perhaps the greatest gift of forgiveness was the restoration of my faith—in myself, in others, and in the divine. Through the act of forgiveness, I found healing and redemption, paving the way for deeper connections and more meaningful relationships. I learned that true forgiveness isn't just about letting go of the past, but about opening oneself up to the endless possibilities of love and grace.

The act of forgiveness taught me that the path to healing begins with a single step—a willingness to let go of the past and embrace the promise of a brighter tomorrow. And though the road may be long and winding, I walk it with courage, knowing that each step brings me closer to the peace and wholeness I seek.

In continuing my journey of forgiveness, I've encountered moments of doubt and resistance. There were times when I questioned whether I was truly capable of letting go of such deep-seated hurt and resentment. But with each challenge, I reminded myself of the transformative power of forgiveness—that it's not just about the other person, but about freeing myself from the chains of bitterness and anger.

I found solace in the teachings of forgiveness shared by spiritual leaders and mentors, drawing strength from their wisdom and guidance. Through prayer, meditation, and reflection, I sought to cultivate a heart that was open and receptive to the healing power of forgiveness.

One of the most profound lessons I learned along the way was the importance of self-forgiveness. In my quest to forgive others, I realized that I also needed to extend that same compassion and understanding to myself. I had to acknowledge my own flaws and mistakes, and forgive myself for any perceived shortcomings or failures. This act of self-compassion was essential in breaking free from the cycle of self-blame and guilt, allowing me to embrace a greater sense of self-love and acceptance.

With time, I discovered that it's not a destination, but a lifelong practice—a continual surrendering of the ego and a commitment to love and grace. It's about choosing compassion over judgment, understanding over resentment, and healing over hurt.

And while the scars of past wounds may still linger, I've come to see them not as reminders of pain, but as symbols of resilience and growth. They serve as a testament to my capacity to overcome adversity and emerge stronger and more compassionate than before.

In the end, forgiveness is a deeply personal and transformative journey—one that requires courage, humility, and a willingness to let go of the past. But through the act of forgiveness, I've discovered a profound sense of freedom and liberation—a freedom to live with an open heart and a spirit unburdened by the weight of unforgiveness. And for that, I am eternally grateful.

It's A Journey

In continuing my journey of forgiveness, I've encountered moments of doubt and resistance. There were times when I questioned whether I was truly capable of letting go of such deep-seated hurt and resentment. But with each challenge, I reminded myself of the transformative power of forgiveness—that it's not just about the other person, but about freeing myself from the chains of bitterness and anger.

I found solace in the teachings of forgiveness shared by spiritual leaders and mentors, drawing strength from their wisdom and guidance. Through prayer, meditation, and reflection, I sought to cultivate a heart that was open and receptive to the healing power of forgiveness.

One of the most profound lessons I learned along the way was the importance of self-forgiveness. In my quest to forgive others, I realized that I also needed to extend that same compassion and understanding to myself. I had to acknowledge my own flaws and mistakes, and forgive myself for any perceived shortcomings or failures. This act of self-compassion was essential in breaking free from the cycle of self-blame and guilt, allowing me to embrace a greater sense of self-love and acceptance.

As I continued to journey towards forgiveness, I discovered that it's not a destination, but a lifelong practice—a continual surrendering of the ego and a commitment to love and grace. It's about choosing compassion over judgment, understanding over resentment, and healing over hurt.

And while the scars of past wounds may still linger, I've come to see them not as reminders of pain, but as symbols of resilience and growth. They serve as a testament to my capacity to overcome adversity and emerge stronger and more compassionate than before.

Forgiveness is a deeply personal and transformative journey—one that requires courage, humility, and a willingness to let go of the past. But through the act of forgiveness, I've discovered a profound sense of freedom and liberation—a freedom to live with an open heart and a spirit unburdened by the weight of unforgiveness. And for that, I am eternally grateful.

It's important to recognize that these actions not only impact our spiritual well-being but also have profound effects on our relationships and interactions with others.

When we forgive those who have wronged us and offer prayers on their behalf, we are participating in a divine exchange of grace and mercy. This act of compassion not only frees us from the bondage of bitterness and resentment but also creates an atmosphere of healing and reconciliation in our relationships.

In Matthew 18:21-22, Jesus instructs Peter about forgiveness, saying, "Then Peter came to Jesus and asked, 'Lord, how many times shall I forgive my brother or sister who sins against me? Up to seven times?' Jesus answered, 'I tell you, not seven times, but seventy-seven times.'" This passage emphasizes the importance of extending forgiveness repeatedly, reflecting the limitless grace and mercy that God extends to us.

Forgiveness is not always easy. It requires humility, patience, and a willingness to let go of the desire for revenge or retribution. However, when we choose to forgive, we emulate the character of Christ and open ourselves up to the transformative power of love and grace.

In addition to forgiveness, prayer plays a crucial role in our spiritual journey and our relationships with others. In James 5:16, it says, "Therefore confess your sins to each other and pray for each other so that you may be healed. The prayer of a righteous person is powerful and effective." This verse highlights the healing power of prayer and the importance of interceding for one another in love.

When we pray for those who have wronged us, we not only release them into God's hands but also invite His love and grace to work in their lives. Prayer has the ability to soften hearts, mend broken relationships, and bring about reconciliation in ways that we may not even comprehend.

Moreover, as we align our prayers with God's will, we can trust that He will bring about justice and redemption in His perfect timing. As it says in Romans 8:28, "And we know that in all things God works for the good of those who love him, who have been called according to his purpose." Even in the midst of pain and injustice, we can have faith that God is at work, bringing about His purposes for our lives and the lives of those around us.

Forgiveness and prayer are powerful spiritual disciplines that have the ability to transform our hearts, our relationships, and our communities. As we choose to forgive others and pray for them, we participate in God's redemptive work in the world, ushering in His kingdom of love, grace, and reconciliation.

Forgiveness and prayer are not just abstract concepts but are deeply intertwined with our everyday lives and experiences. As we continue to explore their significance, it's essential to understand how these practices can manifest in practical ways, shaping our thoughts, words, and actions.

Forgiveness is often described as a journey—a process of letting go and releasing the grip of past hurts and grievances. It requires a deliberate choice to extend grace and mercy to those who have wronged us, even when it feels undeserved. This journey may involve acknowledging our own pain, confronting difficult emotions, and seeking healing and reconciliation.

Prayer, on the other hand, is our direct line of communication with God—an opportunity to pour out our hearts, express gratitude, seek guidance, and intercede for others. Through prayer, we invite God into every aspect of our lives, trusting in His wisdom, love, and sovereignty.

When we combine forgiveness with prayer, we create a powerful synergy—one that has the potential to transform not only our own hearts but also the world around us. By praying for those who have hurt us, we demonstrate our commitment to love and reconciliation, even in the face of adversity. We acknowledge our shared humanity and recognize that we are all in need of God's grace and forgiveness.

Moreover, praying for our enemies is a radical act of defiance against the cycle of hatred and violence that plagues our world. Instead of responding with anger or retaliation, we respond with love and compassion, following the example set by Jesus himself. In Luke 6:27-28, Jesus says, "But to you who are listening I say: Love your enemies, do good to those who hate you, bless those who curse you, pray for those who mistreat you."

This commandment challenges us to break free from the chains of bitterness and resentment and embrace a higher standard of love and grace. It's not about condoning or excusing wrongdoing but about refusing to let hatred and division have the final word. As we pray for our enemies, we invite God to work in their hearts, bringing about transformation and redemption.

Forgiveness and prayer are not passive acts but are powerful tools for change and healing. When we choose to forgive and pray for those who have wronged us, we participate in God's kingdom work, bringing about reconciliation and restoration in our own lives and in the world around us. It's a journey that requires courage, humility, and faith—but one that ultimately leads to freedom, wholeness, and abundant life.

Trying To Forgive And Forget

The pain of losing a loved one is already overwhelming, but experiencing betrayal and abandonment during such a vulnerable time can deepen the wounds in unimaginable ways. When my late husband, Mack, passed away, I was confronted with the stark reality of who truly stood by us in our darkest hour and who chose to turn a blind eye to our grief.

It was a devastating realization to witness the silence of those who had been a part of our lives for years, the ones we had considered friends. Their absence at the funeral, their lack of communication, and their failure to offer even a simple word of condolence felt like a betrayal of the deepest kind. It was as if their friendship had been conditional, contingent upon the good times but nonexistent in times of adversity. Conditional as long as we attended church with them and was considered a part of their fold.

What compounded the pain was the knowledge that some of these individuals had not only neglected to offer their support but had also contributed to my late husband's sense of inadequacy and exclusion. They had belittled his worth, undermined his efforts, and perpetuated a culture of elitism and exclusivity that left him feeling unworthy and marginalized. I watched him struggle with the unspoken feelings of exclusion and people deliberately trying to make him feel inferior.

I found myself grappling with a profound sense of disillusionment and anger. How could people who claimed to be our friends and christians, behave with such callousness and indifference? How could they prioritize their own agendas and egos over extending a simple gesture of compassion and solidarity?

In the midst of my grief and anger, I turned to prayer for solace and guidance. I poured out my heart to God, expressing my pain, my confusion, and my righteous indignation. And in those moments of prayer, I found the strength to release the burden of bitterness and resentment that threatened to consume me.

But forgiveness did not come easily or quickly. It was a deliberate and often painful process—a choice I had to make again and again, despite the lingering scars of betrayal. I had to confront the reality that holding onto anger and resentment only perpetuated the cycle of pain and toxicity. So, I chose to forgive—not for their sake, but for mine.

Yet, even as I forgave, I could not forget. The wounds they inflicted ran deep, leaving lasting scars on my heart and soul. And while I no longer harbored ill will towards them, I could not bring myself to respect or trust them again. Their actions had revealed their true character, and I could not simply overlook or excuse their betrayal. As I write this, I still feel pain. Pain for my late husband and what he struggled with. I find solace in knowing he is resting now and no one can harm him. His breath is with God. He was a good man and did not deserve to be treated the way they treated him. He was a humble man and many opposed him.

IN THE END, I FOUND solace in the belief that justice ultimately belongs to God. He sees the truth of every heart and will hold each person to account for their actions. While I may never receive the closure or apology I desire from those who wronged us, I trust that God's judgment is just and righteous.

In the face of betrayal and exclusion, I am reminded of the importance of standing firm in my convictions and refusing to be swayed by the opinions or actions of others. I refuse to participate in the toxic culture of exclusivity and elitism that seeks to divide and diminish others. Instead, I choose to extend love and compassion to all, regardless of their social status or affiliations. I refuse to be like many of them, hypocritical. It hurts, but I forgive them. Forgiveness does not mean the pain will completely go away.

As I continue to navigate the complexities of grief and healing, I cling to the hope that God's grace is sufficient to sustain me through every trial and tribulation. And though the road ahead may be fraught with challenges and uncertainties, I trust that God's love will guide me and strengthen me, enabling me to emerge from the darkness into the light of His everlasting grace.

In the aftermath of such profound loss and betrayal, I've come to realize that the journey of forgiveness is not linear—it's a process marked by moments of progress and setbacks, of healing and relapse. There are days when the pain feels fresh, when the memories of betrayal threaten to overwhelm me once again. And in those moments, I have to remind myself of the choice I've made—to forgive, to release, and to reclaim my peace.

Forgiveness, I've learned, is not about excusing or justifying the actions of others. It's about acknowledging the pain they've caused while refusing to let it define my identity or dictate my future. It's about reclaiming my power and autonomy in the face of adversity, refusing to be held captive by the hurtful words and actions of others.

At the same time, forgiveness does not mean forgetting. The wounds of betrayal may heal over time, but the scars remain as a testament to the strength and resilience that lies within. I carry these scars with me as a reminder of the battles I've fought and the victories I've won—not in spite of the pain, but because of it.

In my journey of forgiveness, prayer has been my steadfast companion—a source of strength, comfort, and guidance in times of need. Through prayer, I've found the courage to confront my pain, to release my anger, and to extend grace to those who've wronged me. It's a lifeline that connects me to the divine, anchoring me in a reality that transcends the temporal and the ephemeral.

As I continue to navigate the complexities of grief and forgiveness, I find solace in the knowledge that I am not alone. God walks beside me, His presence a constant source of reassurance and support. He sees the depths of my heart, the pain that words cannot express, and He holds me tenderly in His embrace.

In essence, forgiveness is a deeply personal and transformative journey—a journey that leads us from darkness into light, from despair into hope. It's a journey marked by grace, mercy, and love—a journey that ultimately sets us free to embrace the fullness of life and love that God intends for us.

And though the road ahead may be long and arduous, I walk it with faith and determination, knowing that with God's help, all things are possible. For in Him, I find the strength to forgive, to heal, and to live fully and abundantly, no matter what challenges may come my way,

The journey of forgiveness is a sacred and transformative one—a journey that leads us from darkness into light, from despair into hope. It's a journey that requires courage, humility, and faith, but one that ultimately leads to freedom, healing, and wholeness. And as we extend forgiveness to others, may we also receive the gift of forgiveness ourselves—a gift that restores, redeems, and reconciles us to the heart of God.

Indeed, the journey of forgiveness is far from a quick fix or a magical solution to our pain and struggles. It's not a genie-in-a-bottle scenario where we make a wish and poof, all is well. Some days, the weight of our hurt and resentment may feel so heavy that it seems impossible to carry on. And yes, there are moments when we may falter, when old wounds reopen, and when we find ourselves back at square one.

I won't sugarcoat it—it's tough. It's a battle against our own human nature, against the temptation to hold onto grudges and seek retribution. And if we try to go at it alone, relying solely on our own strength and willpower, we'll likely find ourselves falling short time and time again.

But here's the thing—we're not meant to do this alone. That's the crux of it. We were never designed to bear the weight of our pain and resentment on our own shoulders. When we recognize this truth, when we humble ourselves and acknowledge our need for divine intervention, everything changes.

When we submit and surrender our burdens to God, when we ask for His help and strength to overcome our struggles, He is faithful to answer. Every. Single. Time. It's not about summoning a magical solution out of thin air; it's about tapping into the infinite resources of grace and mercy that God freely offers to all who seek Him.

In those moments of surrender, when we lay down our pride and our stubbornness, God meets us right where we are. He extends His hand to lift us up, His arms to embrace us, and His love to heal us. And with His help, we find the strength to keep pressing forward, one step at a time.

But here's the beauty of it—when we realize that we're not alone in this battle, when we embrace the truth that God is fighting alongside us, it ceases to be a battle at all. It becomes a day-by-day process—a journey of growth, healing, and transformation.

So, yes, forgiveness is hard. It's messy, it's painful, and it requires us to confront the darkest corners of our hearts. But with God's help, it's possible. It's possible to find freedom from the shackles of resentment, to experience healing in the midst of our pain, and to walk in the light of His love and grace.

And so, I encourage you—don't try to go it alone. Don't rely solely on your own strength and understanding. Instead, lean into the arms of the One who loves you unconditionally, who knows your pain intimately, and who longs to walk with you every step of the way. For with God, all things are possible, and His grace is more than sufficient to carry you through even the darkest of nights.

As we continue on this journey of forgiveness, we must remind ourselves daily of our dependence on God's grace and strength. It's a conscious choice we make each day to surrender our hurts and grievances to Him, trusting that He will carry us through the challenges and temptations that arise.

In moments of weakness, when the temptation to hold onto bitterness and resentment feels overwhelming, we can turn to God in prayer, seeking His guidance and assistance. We can ask Him to strengthen our resolve, to fill our hearts with His love and compassion, and to help us see others through His eyes.

And when we stumble and fall—as we inevitably will—we can rest assured knowing that God's grace is more than sufficient to cover our failings. His love is unconditional, His forgiveness boundless, and His mercy endless. All we need to do is turn to Him with humble hearts, acknowledging our need for His help and trusting in His faithfulness to uphold us.

But forgiveness is not just about letting go of past hurts; it's also about embracing a mindset of love and compassion toward others. It's about extending the same grace and mercy to others that we ourselves have received from God.

In Matthew 6:14-15, Jesus says, "For if you forgive other people when they sin against you, your heavenly Father will also forgive you. But if you do not forgive others their sins, your Father will not forgive your sins." These words serve as a powerful reminder of the importance of forgiveness in the life of a believer.

When we choose to forgive others, we not only free ourselves from the burden of bitterness and resentment, but we also open the door for God's blessings to flow into our lives. Forgiveness is a key that unlocks the door to healing, reconciliation, and restoration—not just for ourselves, but for all involved.

So let us continue on this journey of forgiveness with courage and perseverance, knowing that God is with us every step of the way. Let us extend grace to others as freely as we have received it ourselves, and let us walk in the light of His love and mercy, shining as beacons of hope and reconciliation in a world that so desperately needs it.

As we press forward on the path of forgiveness, it's important to acknowledge that the journey is not always straightforward or easy. There will be moments of doubt, moments of pain, and moments when the wounds of the past threaten to reopen. But in those moments, we must hold fast to the truth that God's grace is greater than our struggles, and His love is stronger than our pain.

Forgiveness is a process—a journey of the heart that unfolds over time. It's not something that happens all at once, but rather something that we must continually choose, day after day. And while the road may be long and winding, we can take comfort in the knowledge that we do not walk it alone. God is with us, guiding us, strengthening us, and carrying us through every trial and tribulation.

In Psalm 51:10, David cries out to God, saying, "Create in me a pure heart, O God, and renew a steadfast spirit within me." This prayer serves as a reminder that true forgiveness begins in the heart—a heart that is open and receptive to God's transforming love and grace. When we allow God to work in us and through us, He can create something beautiful out of the brokenness of our past.

But forgiveness is not just about letting go of past hurts; it's also about embracing a future filled with hope and possibility. It's about releasing the grip of bitterness and resentment and opening ourselves up to the endless possibilities of grace and redemption.

In Colossians 3:13, we are urged to "Bear with each other and forgive one another if any of you has a grievance against someone. Forgive as the Lord forgave you." This verse reminds us of the incredible gift of forgiveness that we have received from God—an undeserved gift that we are called to extend to others.

And so, as we continue on this journey of forgiveness, let us remember that we are not defined by our past hurts or failures. We are beloved children of God, created in His image and called to love and forgive as He has loved and forgiven us.

May we find the strength to release the burdens of bitterness and resentment, and may we embrace the freedom and joy that comes from walking in the light of God's love. And may we be vessels of His grace and mercy, shining beacons of hope and reconciliation in a world that so desperately needs it.

When They Aren't Sorry

It's a heavy burden to bear when someone hurts you and shows no remorse. I've been there, feeling the weight of their actions pressing down on me while they go about their lives, seemingly unaffected. As a Christian, the concept of forgiveness is ingrained in me, even when it feels impossible. It's not about excusing their behavior or letting them off the hook; it's about releasing myself from the grip of bitterness and anger. But how do you forgive someone who doesn't even ask for it? How do you move forward without the closure of an apology?

For me, it starts with recognizing that forgiveness is more about my own healing than it is about absolving the other person. It's a process, not a one-time event. I have to remind myself daily to let go of the resentment and the desire for retribution. It's not easy, and it doesn't happen overnight, but with prayer and perseverance, it becomes possible.

As I stated earlier, forgiveness doesn't mean forgetting or pretending like nothing happened. It's okay to remember the hurt; it's a part of my story, but it doesn't have to define me. Instead of dwelling on the past, I try to focus on the present and the future. I surround myself with supportive people who lift me up and remind me of my worth. And when those thoughts of anger and betrayal resurface, I turn to prayer to find peace and strength.

As for confronting the person who wronged me, sometimes it's best to let it go and move on. Confrontation may only reignite old wounds and lead to more pain. But if the opportunity presents itself and I feel called to speak my truth, I approach it with grace and humility, remembering that my goal is not retaliation but reconciliation.

In the end, forgiveness is a choice—one that I make for my own well-being and spiritual growth. It's not always easy, and I may stumble along the way, but I trust in God's guidance and the power of love to see me through.

Despite the lack of apology, I've learned that forgiving doesn't mean allowing the same hurtful behavior to continue unchecked. Boundaries are crucial for self-preservation. So, while I extend forgiveness, I also take steps to protect myself from further harm. It's about finding a balance between compassion and self-respect.

When faced with the challenge of forgiving someone who remains unapologetic, I draw strength from the teachings of Jesus. He endured unimaginable suffering and yet still offered forgiveness to those who wronged him, even from the cross. His example reminds me that forgiveness is not a sign of weakness but of profound strength and love.

Forgiveness is not a denial of the pain or an endorsement of the wrongdoing; it's a choice to let go of the past and embrace the possibility of a better future. It's a journey toward freedom from the shackles of resentment and bitterness. And while it may be one of the hardest things I'll ever do, I believe it's also one of the most transformative.

In the end, forgiveness is as much for me as it is for the person who hurt me. By releasing the burden of anger and resentment, I reclaim my peace and my power. I refuse to let someone else's actions define my life or dictate my happiness. Instead, I choose to walk in the light of forgiveness, trusting that God's grace will guide me every step of the way.

Forgiveness isn't a solitary act—it's a continual process of renewal and growth. Each day brings its own challenges and opportunities to extend grace, both to others and to myself. It's about choosing compassion over bitterness, love over hate, and hope over despair.

When faced with the pain of betrayal and the absence of remorse, I remind myself that forgiveness is not a quick fix or an easy solution. It requires patience, humility, and a willingness to let go of the need for vindication. It's about surrendering my desire for justice into the hands of a higher power and trusting in the divine wisdom that surpasses my own understanding.

As I navigate the complexities of forgiveness, I find solace in the knowledge that I am not alone. Countless others have walked this path before me, drawing strength from their faith and their community. I lean on their wisdom and their support, knowing that together, we can overcome even the greatest of hurts.

Ultimately, forgiveness is a testament to the resilience of the human spirit and the transformative power of love. It's a radical act of defiance against the darkness of the world, a declaration that no matter how deep the wounds, healing is always possible. And as I continue on this journey of forgiveness, I do so with an open heart and a steadfast faith, knowing that God's grace will carry me through to a place of peace and wholeness.

Forgiving someone doesn't mean subjecting yourself to further harm or allowing them to continue disrespecting your boundaries. It's about reclaiming your power and asserting your worth. By setting clear boundaries and refusing to tolerate toxic behavior, you teach others how to treat you with respect and dignity.

Moving forward, I've learned to recognize the warning signs of toxic relationships and to trust my instincts when something doesn't feel right. I refuse to be a doormat for those who would take advantage of my kindness or manipulate my emotions for their own gain. I am no longer willing to entertain people who only offer conditional affection or who are quick to betray my trust at the first opportunity.

Instead, I surround myself with genuine, authentic connections—people who lift me up, support me, and celebrate my successes without envy or resentment. I prioritize relationships built on mutual trust, honesty, and integrity, where I can be my true self without fear of judgment or betrayal.

By taking back control of my life and refusing to tolerate toxic behavior, I am reclaiming my power and creating a healthier, more fulfilling future for myself. I am no longer a victim of circumstance but a survivor who refuses to let past hurts define my present or dictate my future.

In essence, forgiving someone doesn't mean forgetting or condoning their actions; it means releasing the hold they have over you and refusing to let their behavior continue to impact your life. It's about choosing to prioritize your own well-being and happiness above all else. And by setting firm boundaries and surrounding yourself with positive influences, you create a safe space where love and respect can flourish, free from the toxicity of betrayal and backstabbing.

In this journey of reclaiming my power and setting healthy boundaries, I've come to understand the importance of self-love and self-respect. It's not selfish to prioritize my own well-being; it's essential for my mental, emotional, and spiritual health.

I've learned to value myself enough to walk away from relationships and situations that no longer serve me or bring me joy. I refuse to tolerate mistreatment or disrespect in any form, knowing that I deserve better. This doesn't mean I harbor resentment or hold grudges; rather, it's a recognition of my own worth and a commitment to honoring that worth in every aspect of my life.

By loving and respecting myself, I set a powerful example for others to follow. I show them that I won't settle for anything less than the love and respect I deserve. And by modeling healthy boundaries and self-care, I empower those around me to do the same in their own lives.

Moving forward, I choose to focus on building meaningful connections with people who value and appreciate me for who I am. I surround myself with individuals who uplift and inspire me, who encourage me to grow and evolve into the best version of myself. And

I cultivate a sense of inner peace and fulfillment that can't be shaken by the actions of others.

In this way, forgiveness becomes not just a personal journey but a transformative act of self-love and empowerment. It's about taking back control of my life and refusing to let past hurts define my future. It's about embracing the power of forgiveness to heal old wounds and create space for new beginnings.

So, even though I may forgive those who have wronged me, I refuse to allow them to continue to harm me. I stand firm in my boundaries and my self-worth, knowing that I am deserving of love, respect, and happiness. And as I move forward on this journey of forgiveness and self-discovery, I do so with confidence, knowing that I am strong, resilient, and worthy of all the good things life has to offer. As the young people say, "you ain't gone play in my face".

The Pain Of Secrets

The journey of forgiveness can be incredibly complex and challenging, especially when the wounds run deep and the pain feels insurmountable. I've witnessed firsthand the struggles of individuals who have endured unimaginable trauma, whether it's the horror of rape, molestation, the loss of a loved one to murder, or the physical and emotional scars of assault. These experiences can leave lasting scars that linger long after the initial wounds have healed.

What makes forgiveness even more difficult is when the perpetrator is someone close to the victim—a family member, a trusted friend, or a respected figure in the community. In these cases, the victim may feel silenced or pressured to keep the abuse hidden, especially if the perpetrator holds a position of power or influence. The fear of judgment, shame, or retaliation can make it nearly impossible for the victim to speak out or seek justice.

I've seen how families can become enmeshed in a web of secrets and denial, perpetuating cycles of abuse and dysfunction across generations. Instead of supporting the victim and holding the perpetrator accountable, family members may choose to protect the abuser, sweeping the abuse under the rug and leaving the victim to suffer in silence.

This culture of silence and secrecy only serves to deepen the wounds and prolong the cycle of pain. It creates a toxic environment where victims are denied the opportunity to heal and perpetrators are allowed to continue their abusive behavior unchecked. And as these unresolved traumas fester beneath the surface, they can manifest in destructive ways, perpetuating a cycle of pain and dysfunction that spans generations.

Breaking free from this cycle requires courage, strength, and a willingness to confront the painful truths that have been buried for so long. It means speaking out against injustice, even when it's uncomfortable or unpopular. It means challenging the status quo and demanding accountability from those who have caused harm.

But perhaps most importantly, it means extending compassion and empathy to both the victims and the perpetrators, recognizing that hurt people hurt people. It means understanding that forgiveness is not about excusing or condoning the abuse, but about freeing oneself from the burden of resentment and anger.

In my own journey of forgiveness, I've learned that healing is possible, even in the face of unspeakable pain. It may take time, and it may require support from trusted friends, family members, or mental health professionals. But with patience, perseverance, and a willingness to confront the past, it is possible to break free from the chains of trauma and reclaim a sense of peace and wholeness. I was almost a victim to something similar, but God protected me and blocked it.

So, to anyone who has experienced the depths of trauma and pain, know that you are not alone. Your experiences are valid, and your voice matters. You deserve love, respect, and healing, and you have the power to break free from the cycle of abuse and dysfunction. You are worthy of forgiveness, both from others and from yourself. And as you continue on your journey of healing and self-discovery, may you find the strength and courage to forgive, to heal, and to reclaim your power.

One of the most heartbreaking aspects of these cycles is the way they can silence and invalidate the experiences of victims, particularly when the abuser holds a position of authority or respect within the family or community. Victims may be made to feel as though their pain is insignificant or unworthy of attention, leading to a sense of isolation and shame that only serves to compound their suffering.

In many cases, the trauma of abuse is compounded by the failure of family members or authorities to acknowledge or address the abuse. Victims may be met with disbelief, blame, or even retaliation when they attempt to speak out, further reinforcing the message that their pain is not valid or worthy of consideration.

This culture of denial and silence can have devastating consequences for victims, leaving them feeling trapped and powerless in the face of their suffering. Without validation and support, they may struggle to find healing or closure, instead carrying the weight of their trauma with them for years, or even a lifetime.

Breaking free from these cycles requires a collective effort to confront and dismantle the systems of power and privilege that allow abuse to flourish unchecked. It means challenging the narratives of shame and silence that have kept victims silenced and marginalized for far too long. It means creating spaces where victims feel safe and supported to speak their truth, free from judgment or retaliation.

But perhaps most importantly, breaking free from these cycles requires a commitment to empathy and compassion—to truly listening to the voices of survivors and honoring their experiences with dignity and respect. It means recognizing that healing is a journey, and that each individual's path to forgiveness and healing is unique.

So, to anyone who has been caught in the grip of generational cycles of abuse and dysfunction, know that you are not alone. Your pain is valid, your voice matters, and you deserve love, support, and healing. And as you continue on your journey of forgiveness and healing, may you find the strength and courage to break free from the chains of the past and embrace a future filled with hope and possibility.

In the quest to break free from generational cycles of abuse and dysfunction, it's crucial to address the underlying root causes that perpetuate these harmful patterns. Often, these cycles are fueled by deeply ingrained beliefs and attitudes that normalize violence, control, and manipulation within family systems.

One of the key factors in perpetuating these cycles is the concept of power dynamics within families. In many cases, abuse occurs within a context where one individual holds power and control over others, whether it's a parent, spouse, or other authority figure. This imbalance of power creates an environment where abuse can thrive, as victims may feel powerless to resist or speak out against their abusers.

Moreover, these power dynamics can be reinforced by broader societal norms and expectations that prioritize obedience and loyalty to authority figures, particularly within the family unit. Children, in particular, may be taught to respect and obey their parents without question, even when faced with abuse or mistreatment.

Another contributing factor to generational cycles of abuse is the normalization of violence and dysfunction within family systems. When abuse is treated as a taboo topic or swept under the rug, it sends the message that such behavior is acceptable or inevitable. This normalization can lead to a cycle of silence and denial, where victims may feel unable or unwilling to seek help or speak out against their abusers.

Additionally, the lack of support and resources for victims of abuse can further perpetuate these cycles. Without access to safe spaces or supportive networks, victims may feel isolated and alone in their suffering, making it even more difficult to break free from the cycle of abuse.

Breaking free from these cycles requires a multifaceted approach that addresses both individual and systemic factors. It involves raising awareness about the dynamics of abuse and the impact it has on victims and families. It also requires providing victims with the support and resources they need to seek help and heal from their trauma.

Betrayal and violation within the context of the church is a deeply troubling reality that can leave lasting scars on victims and communities alike. When those who are supposed to be spiritual leaders and guides betray the trust placed in them, the consequences are devastating. Victims of such betrayal often find themselves in a uniquely challenging position, facing barriers to speaking out and seeking justice due to the authority and influence wielded by the perpetrators.

One of the most troubling aspects of betrayal within the church is the inherent power dynamics at play. Spiritual leaders often hold positions of authority and respect within their communities, which can make it incredibly difficult for victims to come forward with their experiences. The fear of retaliation, ostracism, or disbelief can leave victims feeling isolated and powerless, trapped in a cycle of silence and shame.

Moreover, the culture of silence and secrecy that often surrounds instances of abuse within religious institutions can further compound the trauma experienced by victims. When abuse is swept under the rug or denied altogether, it sends the message that victims' experiences are not valid or worthy of attention. This can have devastating effects on victims' mental, emotional, and spiritual well-being, leading to feelings of betrayal, anger, and profound loss of faith.

In many cases, perpetrators of abuse within the church are shielded from accountability by the very institutions they serve. Whether it's due to a desire to protect the reputation of the church or to avoid scandal, victims may find themselves marginalized and disbelieved, while perpetrators are allowed to continue their abusive behavior unchecked. This systemic failure to address and prevent abuse within religious institutions perpetuates a cycle of harm that can have far-reaching consequences for generations to come.

Forgiveness in the face of such betrayal is an incredibly difficult and painful process. It requires confronting the trauma of the past and finding a way to release the anger, bitterness, and resentment that may have taken root in the aftermath of abuse. But forgiveness is not about absolving perpetrators of their actions or excusing the harm they have caused; rather, it's about freeing oneself from the grip of hatred and allowing space for healing to take place.

As challenging as it may be, forgiveness is ultimately a transformative act of self-love and empowerment. It's about reclaiming one's power and refusing to let the actions of others dictate one's sense of worth or identity. It's about acknowledging the pain and injustice of the past while choosing to embrace a future filled with hope, compassion, and resilience.

In my own journey of faith and forgiveness, I've grappled with the complexities of betrayal and violation within religious contexts. I've witnessed the profound suffering of victims who have been harmed by those they trusted most, and I've struggled to reconcile my own beliefs with the harsh realities of abuse within the church. But through it all, I've come to understand that forgiveness is not a sign of weakness, but of profound strength and courage.

So, to anyone who has been affected by betrayal and violation within the church, know that you are not alone. Your experiences are valid, your pain is real, and your voice matters. And as you navigate the difficult journey of forgiveness, may you find solace in the knowledge that you are worthy of love, respect, and healing, and that you have the power to reclaim your life and your faith.

Forgiveness within the context of betrayal and violation in the church is a deeply personal and often agonizing journey. It requires confronting painful truths, navigating complex emotions, and grappling with the tension between justice and mercy. As individuals of faith, we are called to forgive those who have wronged us, even when the wounds they've inflicted run deep.

One of the most challenging aspects of forgiveness in cases of church betrayal is the conflict between our spiritual beliefs and our human emotions. On one hand, we are taught to emulate the example of Jesus Christ, who offered forgiveness even to those who crucified him. On the other hand, we are confronted with the raw pain and anger that arises from being betrayed by individuals we once trusted implicitly.

I've found that forgiveness is not a linear process but rather a journey filled with twists and turns, progress and setbacks. There are days when I feel strong and empowered, ready to extend forgiveness to those who have hurt me. And then there are days when the pain feels overwhelming, and the idea of forgiveness seems impossible to grasp.

But through it all, I've come to understand that forgiveness is not about forgetting or excusing the harm that has been done; it's about releasing the hold that anger and resentment have on my heart. It's about acknowledging the humanity of both the victim and the perpetrator, recognizing that we are all flawed and fallible beings in need of grace and compassion.

Also, forgiveness does not mean reconciliation or restoration of trust. It's entirely possible to forgive someone without ever reconciling with them or allowing them back into your life. Setting boundaries and protecting oneself from further harm is an essential part of the forgiveness process, particularly in cases where the perpetrator has shown no remorse or willingness to change their behavior.

In cases where forgiveness feels impossible, it's important to remember that healing is a journey, and it's okay to take things one step at a time. Seeking support from trusted friends, family members, or spiritual advisors can provide a safe space to process emotions and explore the possibility of forgiveness.

Ultimately, forgiveness is a deeply personal and individual decision—one that cannot be rushed or forced. It requires honesty, vulnerability, and a willingness to confront uncomfortable truths. But in the end, it offers the promise of liberation and healing, allowing us to reclaim our power and move forward with grace and resilience.

So, to anyone who is struggling to forgive in the face of betrayal and violation in the church, know that you are not alone. Your pain is valid, your journey is unique, and your capacity for forgiveness is a testament to your strength and resilience. And as you navigate the difficult path ahead, may you find peace, healing, and the courage to extend forgiveness, both to others and to yourself.

Ten Steps To Forgive

1. *Prayer*: Begin by praying for the strength and guidance to embark on the journey of forgiveness. Ask God to help you release any feelings of anger, resentment, or bitterness and to fill your heart with His love and compassion.

Prayer has been a cornerstone of my journey towards forgiveness. In the depths of my pain and anguish, I turned to God, seeking solace, strength, and guidance. I poured out my heart to Him, laying bare the raw emotions that weighed heavily upon me—anger, resentment, bitterness. With each whispered prayer, I felt a stirring within me, a subtle shift in perspective that began to loosen the grip of negativity and bitterness that had held me captive for so long.

Like Job, the ancient figure whose story resonates across the ages, I found solace and insight in the act of praying for others. Despite the trials and tribulations he endured, Job remained steadfast in his faith, turning to God in prayer not only for his own sake but also for the well-being of his friends. In the aftermath of his suffering, Job interceded on behalf of those who had doubted and misunderstood him, offering prayers of forgiveness and reconciliation.

As I reflected on Job's example, I realized the profound power of prayer to transform not only my own heart but also the hearts of those who had wronged me. In praying for them, I relinquished my hold on anger and bitterness, entrusting their fate to a higher power. I surrendered my desire for vengeance and retribution, recognizing that true justice lies in God's hands.

But prayer was not merely a means of releasing negative emotions; it was also a pathway to experiencing God's love and compassion in a tangible way. As I poured out my heart in prayer, I felt His presence surrounding me, enfolding me in His embrace. His love became a balm for my wounded soul, soothing the ache of betrayal and filling me with a sense of peace that surpassed all understanding.

In praying for those who had wronged me, I began to see them through God's eyes—as flawed and fallible human beings in need of His grace and mercy, just like myself. I realized that they, too, were struggling with their own burdens and insecurities, and that their hurtful actions were often borne out of pain and brokenness. In praying for them, I found empathy and compassion replacing the resentment and anger that had once consumed me.

Moreover, prayer became a source of strength and resilience as I navigated the challenges of forgiveness. In moments of weakness and doubt, I turned to God, drawing upon His infinite grace and wisdom to guide me through the process. His presence became a source of comfort and reassurance, reminding me that I was never alone, even in my darkest moments.

Through prayer, I discovered the power of forgiveness to heal and transform—not only myself but also my relationships with others. As I lifted up those who had wronged me in prayer, I felt the walls of hostility and distrust begin to crumble, replaced by a newfound sense of empathy and understanding. Prayer became a bridge to reconciliation, paving the way for healing and restoration in relationships that had been fractured by betrayal and hurt.

In praying for my offenders, I found liberation from the bondage of unforgiveness, reclaiming my power and agency in the process. I realized that forgiveness was not a sign of weakness but of profound strength—a courageous act of defiance against the forces of darkness and despair. Through prayer, I learned to release the burdens of the past and embrace a future filled with hope and possibility.

Indeed, prayer became a transformative force in my journey towards forgiveness—a sacred ritual that allowed me to commune with the divine and tap into the limitless reservoir of grace and compassion that flows from God's heart. In praying for my offenders, I discovered the true meaning of forgiveness—not merely as an act of letting go but as a profound expression of love and reconciliation. And in surrendering my pain and anger to God, I found healing and wholeness beyond measure.

As I continued to delve deeper into the practice of prayer as a means of forgiveness, I found that it wasn't just a one-time event but rather an ongoing process—a journey of the heart that required dedication, perseverance, and faith. Each day, I would set aside time to commune with God, pouring out my heart in prayer and seeking His guidance and strength to navigate the complexities of forgiveness.

One of the most profound aspects of praying for my offenders was the transformation that took place within me. As I lifted up their names to God, I felt a shift in my own spirit—a softening of the hardened edges of my heart, a loosening of the chains that had bound me to my pain and resentment. In releasing my offenders to God's care, I found a sense of freedom and liberation that I had never known before.

Moreover, I began to notice subtle changes in my attitude towards my offenders. Where once there had been bitterness and anger, now there was compassion and empathy. I saw them not as enemies to be defeated but as fellow travelers on the journey of life, struggling with their own burdens and seeking redemption and forgiveness, just like myself.

In praying for my offenders, I also discovered the power of intercession—the ability to stand in the gap on behalf of others and to plead for God's mercy and grace to be poured out upon them. I realized that forgiveness was not just about letting go of past hurts but also about actively seeking the well-being and reconciliation of those who had wronged me. As I prayed for their healing and restoration, I found my own heart opening up to the possibility of reconciliation and renewal.

But perhaps the most profound revelation that came through the practice of prayer was the realization that forgiveness was not just a transaction between myself and my offenders but also a divine exchange between myself and God. In surrendering my pain and anger to Him, I found a sense of peace and wholeness that transcended human understanding. I discovered that true forgiveness was not something that I could manufacture on my own but rather a gift that could only be received through the grace of God.

In the end, prayer became not just a means to an end but a way of life—a continual surrender of my will to God's will, a constant seeking of His presence and guidance in every aspect of my journey. Through prayer, I learned to trust in God's timing and wisdom, knowing that He was working all things together for my good, even in the midst of pain and uncertainty.

As I look back on my journey of forgiveness, I am reminded of the words of Jesus, who taught us to pray for those who persecute us and to bless those who curse us. In following His example, I discovered the transformative power of prayer to heal, restore, and reconcile—to bring light into the darkest corners of human brokenness and to usher in a new era of love and forgiveness. And in the end, I found that prayer was not just a means to forgive but the very essence of forgiveness itself—a sacred communion with the divine that has the power to change hearts, mend relationships, and bring about true and lasting reconciliation.

*2. **Reflect on Scripture***: Turn to the Bible for guidance and inspiration on forgiveness. Reflect on passages such as Matthew 6:14-15, which emphasizes the importance of forgiving others in order to receive forgiveness from God, and Colossians 3:13, which encourages us to bear with one another and forgive as the Lord forgave us.

Turning to Scripture for guidance and inspiration on forgiveness has been an anchor in my journey of healing and reconciliation. The Bible, as the inspired Word of God, holds timeless truths and profound wisdom that speak directly to the human experience of pain, forgiveness, and redemption. In the depths of my struggle to forgive, I found solace and strength in the promises and teachings of Scripture, which offered me a beacon of hope amidst the darkness of my despair.

One of the passages that resonated deeply with me is found in Matthew 6:14-15, where Jesus teaches His disciples about the importance of forgiveness: "For if you forgive other people when they sin against you, your heavenly Father will also forgive you. But if you do not forgive others their sins, your Father will not forgive your sins." These words, spoken by Jesus Himself, underscore the profound connection between our willingness to forgive others and our own experience of receiving forgiveness from God.

Reflecting on this passage, I came to understand that forgiveness is not merely a moral obligation but a spiritual imperative—a fundamental aspect of our relationship with God. Just as we are in constant need of God's forgiveness for our own shortcomings and failures, so too are we called to extend that same forgiveness to others. In doing so, we open ourselves up to the boundless grace and mercy of God, which washes over us and cleanses us from all sin and guilt.

But forgiveness is not just about receiving God's forgiveness for ourselves; it's also about extending that same forgiveness to others, regardless of the depth of their wrongdoing. As Jesus teaches us in Matthew 18:21-22, we are called to forgive not just seven times, but seventy-seven times—a reminder of the limitless nature of God's forgiveness and the boundless love that He calls us to emulate.

Another passage that has been instrumental in my journey of forgiveness is found in Colossians 3:13, which exhorts believers to "bear with each other and forgive one another if any of you has a grievance against someone. Forgive as the Lord forgave you." This verse serves as a powerful reminder of the standard of forgiveness set by Jesus Himself, who, in His infinite mercy, chose to forgive us of our sins and reconcile us to Himself.

Reflecting on this verse, I came to understand that forgiveness is not just a one-time event but a continual attitude of grace and compassion towards others. Just as God has forgiven us of our sins, so too are we called to extend that same forgiveness to those who have wronged us. It's a radical call to love and reconciliation—a call to let go of bitterness and resentment and embrace the transformative power of forgiveness.

In my own journey of forgiveness, these passages served as guiding lights, illuminating the path towards healing and reconciliation. They reminded me of the importance of extending grace and mercy to others, even when it felt impossible or undeserved. They challenged me to let go of my pride and ego and embrace the humility of Christ, who, though innocent, chose to bear the weight of our sins on the cross.

So, reflecting on Scripture helped me to gain a deeper understanding of the nature of forgiveness—not as a transaction or a bargaining chip, but as a divine act of love and mercy that transcends human understanding. It reminded me that forgiveness is not about excusing or minimizing the harm that has been done but about releasing the hold that anger and bitterness have on our hearts and allowing God's grace to flow freely through us.

As I immersed myself in the pages of Scripture, I found myself drawn into the stories of forgiveness and redemption that permeate its pages—from the prodigal son who was welcomed back with open arms by his father to the woman caught in adultery who was shown mercy and compassion by Jesus Himself. These stories served as powerful reminders of the transformative power of forgiveness to heal, restore, and reconcile—to bring about reconciliation where there was once brokenness and division.

In the end, reflecting on Scripture was not just a means to an end but a profound encounter with the living Word of God—a sacred journey of discovery and revelation that continues to shape and transform my understanding of forgiveness to this day. And as I continue to meditate on the timeless truths found within its pages, I am reminded of the unfathomable depth of God's love and the boundless grace that He offers to all who seek Him in faith.

In the midst of my struggles with forgiveness, the Scriptures served as a source of solace and strength, offering timeless wisdom and profound insights into the nature of God's love and mercy. As I continued to reflect on passages such as Matthew 6:14-15 and Colossians 3:13, I found myself drawn deeper into the heart of God, where forgiveness flows freely and unconditionally to all who seek it.

One of the most powerful aspects of reflecting on Scripture was the way it brought to life the stories of forgiveness and redemption that are woven throughout its pages. These stories, drawn from the lives of ordinary men and women who encountered the extraordinary grace of God, served as beacons of hope in the darkness of my despair.

One such story that profoundly impacted me was the parable of the prodigal son found in Luke 15:11-32. In this parable, Jesus tells of a wayward son who squanders his inheritance on reckless living, only to return home in shame and desperation. But instead of meeting him with condemnation and judgment, the father welcomes him back with open arms, running to embrace him and restore him to his rightful place in the family.

As I reflected on this parable, I saw myself mirrored in the prodigal son—lost, broken, and in desperate need of God's grace and forgiveness. Like the prodigal son, I had strayed from the path of righteousness and found myself mired in the consequences of my own sin and rebellion. But just as the father in the parable welcomed his wayward son back with open arms, so too did God extend His mercy and forgiveness to me, despite my unworthiness.

Moreover, reflecting on the parable of the prodigal son helped me to see forgiveness from a new perspective—not as something to be earned or deserved, but as a lavish gift freely given by a loving and compassionate Father. It reminded me that forgiveness is not contingent upon our own merit or worthiness but is rooted in the boundless love and grace of God, who longs to reconcile us to Himself and restore us to wholeness.

Another story that deeply impacted me was the account of Jesus' crucifixion found in Luke 23:34, where, in the midst of His suffering, Jesus prays for forgiveness for those who have crucified Him: "Father, forgive them, for they do not know what they are doing." In this simple yet profound prayer, Jesus exemplifies the radical nature of forgiveness—a forgiveness that transcends human understanding and extends even to those who have wronged us in the most unimaginable ways.

As I meditated on Jesus' words from the cross, I was struck by the depth of His love and compassion for His enemies—the very ones who had mocked, tortured, and crucified Him. His prayer for forgiveness was not conditional upon their repentance or remorse but was a selfless act of grace and mercy that flowed freely from a heart overflowing with love.

Moreover, reflecting on Jesus' prayer for forgiveness challenged me to reexamine my own attitudes towards those who had wronged me. If Jesus, in the midst of His own suffering, could extend forgiveness to His enemies, then who was I to withhold forgiveness from those who had wronged me? His example inspired me to let go of my own feelings of anger and resentment and to embrace the radical love and forgiveness that He offers to all who come to Him in faith.

In addition to these stories, reflecting on Scripture also provided me with practical wisdom and guidance on how to cultivate a spirit of forgiveness in my own life. Passages such as Ephesians 4:32, which exhorts believers to "be kind and compassionate to one another, forgiving each other, just as in Christ God forgave you," reminded me of the importance of extending grace and compassion to others, even when it feels difficult or undeserved.

Similarly, passages such as Romans 12:17-21, which instructs believers to "do not repay anyone evil for evil...Do not be overcome by evil, but overcome evil with good," challenged me to rise above the cycle of retaliation and vengeance and to respond to wrongdoing with love and forgiveness. These passages served as practical guides for navigating the complexities of forgiveness in real-life situations, offering wisdom and insight into how to respond to hurt and betrayal with grace and humility.

In the end, reflecting on Scripture was not just a mental exercise but a deeply spiritual practice—an encounter with the living Word of God that transformed my heart and mind in profound ways. Through the stories, teachings, and wisdom found within its pages, I discovered the transformative power of forgiveness to heal, restore, and reconcile—to bring light into the darkest corners of human brokenness and to usher in a new era of love and forgiveness. And as I continue to meditate on the timeless truths found within its pages, I am reminded of the unfathomable depth of God's love and the boundless grace that He offers to all who seek Him in faith.

3. *Acknowledge the Hurt*: Allow yourself to acknowledge the pain and suffering caused by the offense. It's essential to confront the depth of your emotions and recognize the impact of the wrongdoing on your life.

Acknowledging the hurt caused by the offense has been a crucial step in my journey towards forgiveness. It's been a deeply personal and often painful process, one that has required me to confront the depth of my emotions and come to terms with the impact of the wrongdoing on my life.

At first, I found it difficult to acknowledge the hurt I was feeling. There was a part of me that wanted to push it aside, to bury it deep down and pretend like it didn't exist. I thought that by ignoring my pain, I could somehow make it go away. But the truth is, pain doesn't just disappear on its own—it demands to be felt, acknowledged, and processed.

So I made the decision to face my pain head-on—to sit with it, to wrestle with it, and to allow myself to fully experience the depth of my emotions. And as I did, I began to realize just how profound the impact of the offense had been on my life. It wasn't just a surface-level hurt—it was a deep, visceral pain that permeated every aspect of my being.

I felt betrayed—betrayed by someone I had trusted, someone I had opened up to, someone I had allowed into the innermost recesses of my heart. The realization that this person had wronged me, had violated my trust and betrayed my confidence, cut me to the core. It shattered my sense of security and left me feeling vulnerable and exposed.

I felt anger—anger at the injustice of it all, anger at the pain and suffering that had been inflicted upon me, anger at the sheer audacity of the offense. How could someone do something so hurtful, so callous, so utterly devoid of compassion? The anger burned inside me like a raging fire, consuming everything in its path.

I felt sadness—sadness for the loss of what could have been, sadness for the shattered dreams and broken promises, sadness for the innocence that had been stolen from me. The weight of my sadness felt like a heavy burden, pressing down on me and threatening to crush me beneath its weight.

But amidst the pain and suffering, I also felt something else—something unexpected and profound. I felt a glimmer of hope—a tiny spark of light shining in the darkness. It was the realization that even in my darkest hour, even in the depths of my despair, I was not alone. God was with me, walking beside me every step of the way, offering His comfort, His strength, and His unfailing love.

As I allowed myself to acknowledge the hurt I was feeling, I began to see it not as a sign of weakness but as a testament to my strength. It takes courage to confront pain, to sit with it, to allow yourself to be vulnerable. And in acknowledging my pain, I was taking the first step towards healing—a step towards reclaiming my power and my agency in the face of adversity.

Moreover, acknowledging the hurt allowed me to release it—to let go of the anger, the sadness, the bitterness that had held me captive for so long. It was a cathartic process, a purging of the toxic emotions that had poisoned my soul and prevented me from moving forward. In acknowledging my pain, I was freeing myself from its grip, opening myself up to the possibility of healing and forgiveness.

But perhaps most importantly, acknowledging the hurt allowed me to honor my own experiences—to validate my own feelings and emotions. Too often, we minimize our own pain, telling ourselves that we shouldn't feel a certain way or that our feelings aren't valid. But the truth is, our feelings matter—they are a reflection of our innermost selves, and they deserve to be acknowledged and respected.

In the end, acknowledging the hurt was not just about confronting the past—it was about embracing the present and laying the foundation for a brighter future. It was about reclaiming my power, my dignity, and my sense of self-worth. And as I continue on my journey towards forgiveness, I know that acknowledging the hurt will be an ongoing process—one that requires courage, compassion, and grace. But I am committed to facing it head-on, knowing that in doing so, I am taking the first step towards true healing and reconciliation.

As I continued to acknowledge the hurt caused by the offense, I realized that it wasn't just a one-time acknowledgment but an ongoing process—a journey of self-discovery and healing that unfolded gradually over time. Each day brought new layers of emotion to the surface, new depths of pain to confront, and new opportunities for growth and transformation.

One of the challenges I faced in acknowledging the hurt was the fear of being overwhelmed by it—of drowning in a sea of sadness, anger, and bitterness. But I soon came to realize that by allowing myself to fully experience my emotions, I was actually empowering myself to heal. Instead of suppressing my feelings, I embraced them, recognizing them as an integral part of my healing journey.

In acknowledging the hurt, I also had to confront the reality of the impact it had on my life. It wasn't just a matter of acknowledging the pain itself but also the ways in which it had affected my relationships, my sense of self-worth, and my ability to trust others. The hurt had left scars—both visible and invisible—that would take time and effort to heal.

Moreover, acknowledging the hurt required me to confront my own role in the situation—to acknowledge my own vulnerabilities, insecurities, and shortcomings. It was a humbling process—one that forced me to take a hard look at myself and the ways in which I had contributed to the dynamics of the offense. But in doing so, I gained a deeper understanding of myself and my own needs, paving the way for greater self-awareness and personal growth.

But perhaps the most challenging aspect of acknowledging the hurt was the need to let go—to release the grip that the offense had on my heart and soul. It was a process of surrender—a relinquishing of control and a surrendering to the healing power of God's grace. In letting go, I found freedom—a freedom to forgive, to love, and to live fully in the present moment.

As I journeyed through the process of acknowledging the hurt, I found that I was not alone. God walked beside me every step of the way, offering His comfort, His strength, and His unfailing love. He became my rock, my refuge, and my source of hope in the midst of the storm. And as I leaned on Him, I found the courage to face my pain, to confront my fears, and to embrace the journey of healing and forgiveness.

In the end, acknowledging the hurt was not just a means to an end but a sacred act of self-love and self-compassion. It was about honoring my own experiences, validating my own feelings, and reclaiming my own power. And as I emerged from the depths of my pain, I discovered a newfound sense of resilience, strength, and grace—a testament to the transformative power of acknowledging the hurt and embracing the journey of healing and forgiveness.

4. *Release Resentment*: Make a conscious decision to release feelings of resentment and bitterness towards the person who hurt you. Remember that holding onto these negative emotions only prolongs your own suffering and hinders your ability to experience peace and healing.

Releasing resentment and bitterness towards the person who hurt me was perhaps one of the most challenging steps in my journey towards forgiveness. It required a conscious decision—a deliberate choice to let go of the negative emotions that had taken root in my heart and soul. But I knew deep down that holding onto these emotions would only prolong my own suffering and hinder my ability to experience true peace and healing.

At first, the idea of releasing resentment felt overwhelming. After all, I had every right to feel angry and bitter towards the person who had wronged me. Their actions had caused me pain and suffering, and it seemed only natural to hold onto those feelings as a form of self-protection. But as time went on, I began to realize that holding onto resentment was like holding onto a burning coal—it only burned me from the inside out, leaving me feeling scorched and wounded.

So I made the conscious decision to release resentment—to loosen my grip on the anger and bitterness that had consumed me for so long. It wasn't easy, and there were times when I felt like I was swimming against the tide, struggling to let go of emotions that seemed to have a vice-like grip on my heart. But with each passing day, I felt a weight being lifted off my shoulders, a burden being lifted from my soul.

One of the things that helped me release resentment was the realization that forgiveness was not about excusing or condoning the wrong that had been done to me. It wasn't about letting the other person off the hook or pretending like the hurt had never happened. Instead, it was about freeing myself from the prison of my own bitterness and reclaiming my power to choose how I wanted to live my life.

I also found strength in the words of Jesus, who taught us to love our enemies and pray for those who persecute us. His example of radical forgiveness, even in the face of unimaginable suffering, inspired me to follow in His footsteps and extend grace and compassion to those who had wronged me. And as I prayed for the person who hurt me, I felt a shift in my heart—a softening of the anger and resentment that had once consumed me.

But perhaps the most powerful realization I had was that releasing resentment was not just about letting go of negative emotions—it was also about making room for love and healing to enter my life. As I released the bitterness that had held me captive for so long, I felt a sense of lightness and freedom wash over me. I began to experience moments of joy and peace that I hadn't felt in years, and I knew that I was on the right path towards true healing and wholeness.

Of course, releasing resentment didn't happen overnight. It was a gradual process—a journey of letting go, one step at a time. There were days when I stumbled and faltered, days when the old wounds reopened and the familiar feelings of anger and bitterness threatened to overwhelm me. But each time I fell, I picked myself up again, dusted myself off, and reminded myself of the importance of releasing resentment for my own sake.

In the end, releasing resentment was a deeply personal and profoundly liberating experience. It was a journey of self-discovery and self-transformation—a journey that led me to a place of greater peace, joy, and compassion. And as I continue to walk this path of forgiveness,

I know that releasing resentment will be an ongoing process—one that requires patience, perseverance, and a willingness to open my heart to the transformative power of love.

As I continued on my journey to release resentment, I encountered moments of both triumph and struggle. It was a process that required patience, self-reflection, and a deep commitment to my own healing and well-being.

One of the key realizations that helped me in releasing resentment was the understanding that holding onto negative emotions only perpetuates my own suffering. As I harbored feelings of anger, bitterness, and resentment towards the person who hurt me, I was essentially allowing them to have power over me. I was giving them control over my emotions and allowing their actions to dictate my state of mind. But by making the conscious decision to release resentment, I was reclaiming my power and taking back control of my own emotional well-being.

Another important aspect of releasing resentment was learning to separate the person from their actions. While it was easy to vilify the individual who had wronged me, I realized that harboring resentment towards them was ultimately counterproductive. I began to recognize that people are multifaceted beings, capable of both good and bad, and that their actions do not define their entire identity. By acknowledging the humanity of the person who hurt me and understanding that they, too, are flawed and imperfect, I was able to cultivate a sense of empathy and compassion towards them.

Practicing forgiveness also required me to shift my perspective from one of victimhood to one of empowerment. Instead of seeing myself as a passive recipient of harm, I began to view forgiveness as an act of strength and resilience. By releasing resentment, I was taking control of my own narrative and refusing to allow the actions of others to define me. I was choosing to rise above the hurt and reclaim my agency in shaping my own destiny.

Moreover, I found that releasing resentment was closely tied to the practice of self-care and self-love. As I let go of negative emotions, I created space within myself for positivity, joy, and healing to flourish. I engaged in activities that brought me happiness and fulfillment, surrounded myself with supportive and loving people, and prioritized my own mental and emotional well-being. By nurturing myself in this way, I was able to cultivate a sense of inner peace and wholeness that transcended the pain of the past.

But perhaps the most profound aspect of releasing resentment was the sense of freedom and liberation it brought into my life. As I let go of the burdensome weight of anger and bitterness, I felt as though a heavy burden had been lifted from my shoulders. I no longer felt shackled by the chains of resentment, but instead, I experienced a newfound sense of lightness and ease. I was able to move through life with a greater sense of clarity, purpose, and joy, unencumbered by the weight of past grievances.

In the end, releasing resentment was a deeply transformative process—one that required courage, humility, and a willingness to embrace vulnerability. It was a journey of self-discovery and self-reclamation, as I learned to let go of the past and embrace the present moment with an open heart and mind. And as I continue on my path of forgiveness, I know that releasing resentment will be an ongoing practice—one that I will continue to cultivate with compassion, grace, and perseverance.

5. ***Choose Forgiveness***: Forgiveness is a choice, not a feeling. Choose to forgive the person who wronged you, even if you don't feel like it at the moment. Trust that God will honor your decision and guide you through the process of forgiveness.

Choosing forgiveness was a pivotal moment in my journey towards healing and reconciliation. It was a decision that required courage, humility, and a deep sense of faith—a willingness to let go of past hurts and embrace the transformative power of grace and mercy.

At first, the idea of choosing forgiveness felt daunting. After all, the wounds inflicted upon me ran deep, and the pain lingered long after the initial offense. It seemed almost impossible to imagine extending forgiveness to the person who had wronged me—to let go of the hurt and anger that had become so deeply ingrained within me.

But as I reflected on the teachings of Scripture and the example of Jesus Christ, I began to understand that forgiveness was not just a fleeting emotion but a deliberate choice—an act of the will that transcended feelings and circumstances. It was a decision to extend grace and mercy to the person who hurt me, even when they didn't deserve it, and to trust in God's ability to bring beauty out of brokenness.

Choosing forgiveness meant acknowledging the humanity of the person who wronged me and recognizing that they, too, were flawed and imperfect beings in need of God's grace. It meant letting go of the desire for revenge or retribution and instead choosing to respond with compassion and empathy. It meant refusing to allow the actions of others to dictate my own state of mind and heart and instead taking ownership of my own emotional well-being.

Choosing forgiveness required me to confront my own pride and ego—to let go of the need to be right or to seek validation from others. It meant humbling myself before God and admitting that I, too, was in need of His forgiveness and mercy. It meant surrendering my desire for justice and instead entrusting the situation into God's hands, knowing that He is the ultimate arbiter of justice and righteousness.

But perhaps the most profound aspect of choosing forgiveness was the sense of liberation and freedom it brought into my life. As I made the conscious decision to forgive, I felt as though a heavy burden had been lifted from my shoulders—a burden of bitterness, resentment, and anger that had weighed me down for far too long. In its place, I experienced a newfound sense of lightness and peace—a peace that surpassed all understanding and filled me with a deep sense of joy and contentment.

Of course, choosing forgiveness was not a one-time event but an ongoing process—a journey of surrender and renewal that unfolded gradually over time. There were moments when old wounds reopened, and the temptation to hold onto bitterness resurfaced. But each time, I reaffirmed my decision to forgive, knowing that it was the only path towards true healing and reconciliation.

As I look back on my decision to choose forgiveness, I am reminded of the words of Jesus, who taught us to love our enemies and pray for those who persecute us. His example of radical forgiveness, even in the face of unimaginable suffering, inspires me to follow in His footsteps and extend grace and compassion to those who have wronged me. And as I continue on my journey of forgiveness, I do so with a deep sense of gratitude and humility, knowing that it is only through God's grace that I am able to extend forgiveness to others.

As I continued to walk the path of forgiveness, I encountered moments of both challenge and triumph. Choosing forgiveness was not a one-time decision but a daily practice—a conscious effort to let go of past hurts and embrace a new way of living.

One of the challenges I faced in choosing forgiveness was the temptation to hold onto resentment and bitterness. There were times when the wounds of the past felt fresh and raw, and the desire for justice or vindication burned within me. In those moments, I had to remind myself of the importance of letting go—of releasing the grip that anger and resentment had on my heart and soul.

I also had to confront my own fears and insecurities—the fear of being vulnerable, the fear of being hurt again, the fear of being seen as weak for choosing to forgive. But I soon came to realize that forgiveness was not a sign of weakness but of strength—a courageous act of love and compassion that required far more courage than holding onto bitterness ever could.

Choosing forgiveness required me to confront the misconceptions and myths surrounding forgiveness—the idea that forgiving meant condoning the wrong that had been done or that it required reconciliation with the person who hurt me. I had to learn that forgiveness was not about excusing or minimizing the harm that had been done but about freeing myself from the prison of resentment and reclaiming my own sense of peace and well-being.

But amidst the challenges, there were also moments of triumph—moments when I felt the transformative power of forgiveness working in my life. As I chose to let go of past hurts and extend grace and compassion to those who had wronged me, I experienced a profound sense of liberation and freedom. I no longer felt shackled by the chains of bitterness and anger but instead felt empowered to live life on my own terms—to love boldly, to forgive freely, and to embrace the fullness of God's grace.

Choosing forgiveness also opened the door to healing and reconciliation in my relationships. As I extended forgiveness to others, I found that it paved the way for healing and restoration—not just in my relationship with them but also within myself. I experienced a newfound sense of peace and wholeness—a peace that surpassed all understanding and a wholeness that could only come from God's grace.

But perhaps the greatest triumph of all was the sense of connection and unity that forgiveness brought into my life. As I chose to forgive others, I discovered that it was not just an individual act but a communal one—a way of building bridges and fostering understanding across divides. I found that forgiveness had the power to break down walls of hostility and division and to create a space for love and reconciliation to flourish.

At the end of the day, choosing forgiveness was a deeply personal and profoundly transformative experience. It was a journey of self-discovery and self-transformation—a journey that led me to a place of greater peace, joy, and wholeness. And as I continue on my path of forgiveness, I do so with a deep sense of gratitude and humility, knowing that it is only through God's grace that I am able to extend forgiveness to others. As the young people say, "I'm not gone be looking old and ugly holding on to unforgiveness'.'.

6. **Pray for the Offender**: Pray for the person who hurt you, asking God to bless them and soften their heart. Praying for your offender can help cultivate compassion and empathy, making it easier to extend forgiveness.

Praying for the person who hurt me was perhaps one of the most challenging yet transformative aspects of my journey towards forgiveness. It required me to set aside my own feelings of anger and resentment and instead extend grace and compassion to someone who had wronged me deeply. But as I began to pray for my offender, I discovered a profound sense of healing and reconciliation that transcended my own understanding.

At first, the idea of praying for someone who had caused me so much pain seemed counterintuitive. After all, why should I pray for someone who had hurt me? Why should I extend kindness and compassion to someone who had shown me none in return? But as I delved deeper into the teachings of Scripture, I began to realize that praying for my offender was not just about them—it was also about me.

One of the key realizations I had was that holding onto anger and resentment was only hurting me in the long run. As I harbored negative emotions towards my offender, I was allowing them to have power over me—power to dictate my thoughts, emotions, and actions. But by choosing to pray for them, I was reclaiming my own sense of agency and autonomy. I was refusing to allow their actions to define me or dictate the course of my life.

Praying for my offender helped me to cultivate a sense of empathy and compassion towards them. As I lifted them up in prayer, I began to see them not as an enemy to be defeated but as a fellow human being in need of God's grace and mercy. I began to understand that they, too, were struggling with their own pain and brokenness and that their actions were likely a reflection of their own inner turmoil.

But perhaps the most profound aspect of praying for my offender was the sense of peace and freedom it brought into my life. As I surrendered my desire for revenge or retribution and instead prayed for their well-being, I felt a weight being lifted off my shoulders—a burden of bitterness, resentment, and anger that had weighed me down for far too long. In its place, I experienced a sense of lightness and ease—a peace that surpassed all understanding and filled me with a deep sense of joy and contentment.

But praying for my offender was not just about asking God to bless them—it was also about asking God to soften their heart and open their eyes to the pain they had caused. It was about inviting God into the midst of our brokenness and asking Him to bring about healing and reconciliation where there was once hurt and division. And as I prayed for my offender, I began to see small glimpses of change—a softening of their heart, a willingness to acknowledge their wrongdoing, and a desire to make amends.

Praying for my offender was a deeply transformative experience—one that brought me closer to God and to myself. It was a journey of surrender and trust—a willingness to let go of my own desires and instead align myself with God's will. And as I continue to pray for my offender, I do so with a deep sense of gratitude and humility, knowing that it is only through God's grace that true healing and reconciliation can take place.

As I continued to pray for my offender, I found that the act of prayer became a lifeline—a source of strength, hope, and healing in the midst of pain and suffering. It was a daily practice—a deliberate choice to lift them up to God and entrust their well-being into His hands.

One of the things that helped me in my prayers was focusing on the humanity of my offender. Instead of seeing them solely as the person who had wronged me, I began to see them as a fellow human being—a complex individual with their own struggles, fears, and insecurities. I realized that they, too, were created in the image of God and deserving of His love and compassion.

As I prayed for my offender, I asked God to bless them—to shower them with His grace and mercy and to guide them along the path of healing and reconciliation. I prayed for their physical, emotional, and spiritual well-being, knowing that they were in need of God's love and provision just as much as I was.

But perhaps the most powerful aspect of my prayers was the sense of connection and empathy it fostered within me. As I lifted my offender up to God, I found that my heart softened towards them, and I began to see them through eyes of compassion and understanding. I realized that they, too, were wounded souls in need of God's grace and forgiveness, and I prayed that they would come to experience the transformative power of His love in their lives.

Moreover, praying for my offender helped me to release any lingering feelings of anger, resentment, or bitterness that I held towards them. It was a way of surrendering my own desire for justice or revenge and instead trusting in God's perfect timing and justice. I knew that vengeance belonged to the Lord and that He would ultimately bring about justice in His own way and in His own time.

But perhaps the greatest gift of praying for my offender was the sense of peace and freedom it brought into my life. As I entrusted their well-being into God's hands, I felt a weight being lifted off my shoulders—a burden of bitterness, resentment, and anger that had held me captive for far too long. In its place, I experienced a sense of lightness and ease—a peace that surpassed all understanding and filled me with a deep sense of joy and contentment.

I realized that praying for my offender or in my case offenders was not just an act of obedience or duty—it was an act of love. It was a way of extending grace and compassion to someone who had wronged me and trusting in God's ability to bring about healing and reconciliation in their lives. And as I continue to pray for my offender, I do so with a deep sense of gratitude and humility, knowing that it is only through God's grace that true forgiveness and reconciliation can take place.

7. ***Practice Empathy***: Try to understand the circumstances and motivations that may have led the person to hurt you. Recognize that everyone is fallible and capable of making mistakes, and extend grace and compassion accordingly.

Practicing empathy, especially towards those who have hurt me, has always been somewhat of an Achilles heel for me. It's a characteristic that I've possessed for as long as I can remember—one that often leaves me feeling torn between my own feelings of hurt and the desire to understand and empathize with the person who caused that hurt. But as I've embarked on my journey of forgiveness, I've come to realize the profound power of empathy in facilitating healing and reconciliation.

At first glance, empathy may seem like a daunting task, especially when directed towards someone who has caused me pain. After all, why should I extend understanding and compassion to someone who has wronged me? Why should I bother trying to see things from their perspective when all I can feel is the sting of their actions?

But as I looked deeper into the concept of empathy, I began to realize that it wasn't about excusing or justifying the wrong that had been done to me. Instead, it was about recognizing the shared humanity that binds us all together—the fact that we are all fallible, imperfect beings in need of grace and understanding.

Practicing empathy meant taking a step back from my own pain and trying to understand the circumstances and motivations that may have led the person to hurt me. It meant recognizing that hurt people hurt people—that often, those who inflict pain are themselves grappling with their own wounds and insecurities. It meant acknowledging that the person who hurt me may have been acting out of fear, anger, or desperation—emotions that clouded their judgment and led them to make hurtful choices.

But perhaps the most profound aspect of practicing empathy was the sense of liberation and freedom it brought into my life. As I extended understanding and compassion to my offender, I found that I was no longer held captive by feelings of anger, resentment, or bitterness. Instead, I experienced a sense of lightness and peace—a peace that surpassed all understanding and filled me with a deep sense of joy and contentment.

I think that practicing empathy allowed me to break free from the cycle of hurt and retaliation that often characterizes human relationships. Instead of responding to pain with more pain, I chose to respond with love—with understanding, compassion, and grace. I recognized that empathy was not just a gift that I extended to others but also a gift that I gave to myself—a gift of healing, reconciliation, and wholeness.

Of course, practicing empathy was not always easy. There were moments when my own pain threatened to overshadow my ability to empathize with others. There were times when I felt tempted to retreat into my own woundedness and shut myself off from the world. But each time, I reminded myself of the transformative power of empathy—the way it had the ability to soften hearts, mend relationships, and bring about healing where there was once hurt.

In the end, practicing empathy was a deeply transformative experience—one that brought me closer to God and to myself. It was a journey of self-discovery and self-transformation—a journey that led me to a place of greater peace, joy, and wholeness. And as I continue to practice empathy in my daily life, I do so with a deep sense of gratitude and humility, knowing that it is only through God's grace that true healing and reconciliation can take place.

I encountered moments of both challenge and growth. Each interaction with my offender presented an opportunity to deepen my understanding and compassion, but it also tested the limits of my own capacity for forgiveness and grace.

One of the challenges I faced in practicing empathy was the temptation to revert to old patterns of thinking and behavior—to allow my own hurt and anger to overshadow my ability to empathize with my offender. There were times when the wounds of the past felt too fresh, too raw, and I struggled to see beyond my own pain. But each time I found myself slipping into this mindset, I reminded myself of the importance of empathy—the way it had the power to transform hearts and mend relationships., practicing empathy required me to confront my own biases and prejudices—the preconceived notions and judgments that clouded my ability to see the humanity in others. It meant setting aside my own ego and opening myself up to the possibility of understanding and connection, even with those who had wronged me. It meant acknowledging that everyone is capable of making mistakes and that no one is beyond redemption.

But perhaps the greatest challenge of all was the need to forgive—not just once, but again and again, as new hurts and offenses arose. It was a constant battle against the impulse to hold onto resentment and bitterness, to close myself off from the possibility of reconciliation and healing. But each time I chose to forgive, I found that my capacity for empathy grew stronger, and my heart became more open to the possibility of redemption.

In the midst of these challenges, however, there were also moments of profound growth and transformation. As I practiced empathy, I found that I was able to see my offender in a new light—not as a villain or an enemy, but as a fellow human being struggling to find their way in the world. I began to recognize the shared humanity that connected us—that we were all broken, imperfect beings in need of grace and understanding.

It allowed me to break free from the cycle of hurt and retaliation that often characterizes human relationships. Instead of responding to pain with more pain, I chose to respond with love—with understanding, compassion, and grace. I recognized that empathy was not just a gift that I extended to others but also a gift that I gave to myself—a gift of healing, reconciliation, and wholeness.

But perhaps the most profound aspect of practicing empathy was the way it deepened my relationship with God. As I sought to understand and empathize with my offender, I found that I was drawn closer to the heart of God—a God who is infinitely compassionate, merciful, and forgiving. I began to see myself and others through His eyes—to recognize the inherent dignity and worth of every human being, regardless of their past mistakes or shortcomings.

In the end, practicing empathy was a journey of self-discovery and transformation—a journey that led me to a deeper understanding of myself, others, and the nature of God's love. And as I continue on this journey, I do so with a renewed sense of purpose and commitment, knowing that empathy has the power to heal, restore, and transform even the most broken of relationships.

8. **Let Go of Grudges:** Release any desire for revenge or retribution. Instead, focus on letting go of past grievances and embracing a spirit of reconciliation and peace.

Letting go of grudges has been one of the most challenging aspects of my journey towards forgiveness. Despite my best efforts to release feelings of anger and resentment, there are times when the memory of past grievances lingers, like a stubborn stain that refuses to fade away. It's as if the wounds inflicted by those who have wronged me are etched into my psyche, serving as constant reminders of the hurt and betrayal I've experienced. In these moments, the temptation to hold onto grudges—to seek revenge or retribution—can be overwhelming. It's a struggle against the tide of bitterness and indignation, a battle to reclaim my peace of mind and embrace a spirit of reconciliation and forgiveness.

One of the greatest challenges I face in letting go of grudges is the persistent memory of past wrongs. It's as if my mind is programmed to replay these memories on an endless loop, dredging up feelings of hurt and resentment each time they resurface. Whether it's a hurtful remark, a betrayal of trust, or a blatant act of injustice, the memory of these past grievances has a way of haunting me, leaving me feeling angry, bitter, and vengeful.

Letting go of grudges requires a willingness to relinquish the desire for revenge or retribution—to resist the urge to retaliate against those who have wronged me. It's a conscious choice to rise above the impulse for retaliation and instead focus on the pursuit of reconciliation and peace. But this is easier said than done, especially when the wounds are still fresh and the pain is still raw. In these moments, it's all too tempting to give in to the temptation for payback—to lash out in anger or seek justice through less-than-noble means.

Another challenge I face in letting go of grudges is the fear of being hurt again. It's as if the scars of past betrayals have left me wary and distrustful, hesitant to let down my guard and open myself up to the possibility of being hurt once more. This fear acts as a barrier to forgiveness, preventing me from fully embracing the spirit of reconciliation and peace. It's a constant struggle to overcome this fear—to step out in faith and extend forgiveness, even when it feels risky or uncertain.

But despite these challenges, I am committed to the journey of letting go of grudges and embracing a spirit of reconciliation and peace. I know that holding onto bitterness and resentment only serves to poison my own heart and soul, robbing me of the joy and freedom that comes from forgiveness. I recognize that forgiveness is not a one-time event but an ongoing process—a journey of surrender and release that requires patience, perseverance, and grace.

One of the things that helps me in letting go of grudges is the practice of mindfulness—of being present in the moment and acknowledging my feelings without judgment or attachment. Instead of allowing myself to be consumed by thoughts of past wrongs, I try to cultivate a sense of detachment, recognizing that holding onto grudges only perpetuates my own suffering. I remind myself that I have the power to choose how I respond to these feelings—to let them go and embrace a spirit of forgiveness and reconciliation.

I find strength in the words of Jesus, who taught us to love our enemies and pray for those who persecute us. His example of radical forgiveness, even in the face of unimaginable suffering, inspires me to follow in His footsteps and extend grace and compassion to those who have wronged me. I draw comfort from His promise that forgiveness is not a sign of weakness but of strength—that in letting go of grudges, we find true freedom and peace.

Letting go of grudges is a journey—a journey of surrender and release, of forgiveness and reconciliation. It's a journey that requires courage, humility, and a willingness to let go of past hurts in order to embrace a future filled with hope and healing. And as I continue on this journey, I do so with a deep sense of gratitude and humility, knowing that it is only through God's grace that I am able to release grudges and embrace a spirit of reconciliation and peace.

As I strive to let go of grudges, I've come to realize that it's a process that requires intentional effort and self-awareness. It's not something that happens overnight, but rather a journey of growth and transformation—a journey that unfolds gradually as I learn to release the grip of bitterness and embrace the possibility of reconciliation.

One of the strategies that has been helpful for me in letting go of grudges is the practice of forgiveness meditation. This involves setting aside time each day to sit quietly and reflect on the people who have wronged me, offering them forgiveness and releasing any feelings of resentment or anger. Through this practice, I cultivate a sense of empathy and compassion towards my offenders, recognizing that they, too, are human beings who are deserving of grace and forgiveness.

Another helpful strategy is journaling. Writing down my thoughts and feelings allows me to process my emotions in a healthy way and gain clarity on the root causes of my grudges. By examining the underlying reasons for my resentment, I can begin to address them more effectively and work towards releasing them. Journaling also provides a record of my progress, allowing me to track my growth and celebrate small victories along the way.

I've also found solace in seeking support from trusted friends, family members, or spiritual mentors. Opening up to others about my struggles with letting go of grudges helps to lighten the burden and provides me with much-needed encouragement and guidance. Their perspective and wisdom often offer new insights and strategies for overcoming resentment and embracing forgiveness.

In addition, I've learned to practice self-compassion and self-care as I navigate the journey of releasing grudges. This involves treating myself with kindness and understanding, especially when I find myself struggling with negative emotions or self-doubt. By prioritizing my own well-being and practicing self-care activities such as exercise, meditation, and relaxation, I replenish my emotional reserves and build resilience in the face of adversity.

Furthermore, I've come to recognize the importance of setting healthy boundaries in my relationships as a means of protecting myself from future hurt. This involves clearly communicating my needs and expectations to others and being assertive in asserting my boundaries. By establishing healthy boundaries, I create a safe and supportive environment for myself, reducing the likelihood of future conflicts and resentments.

Ultimately, letting go of grudges is a deeply personal journey—one that requires courage, humility, and a willingness to confront the pain of the past. It's a journey of self-discovery and self-empowerment, as I reclaim my power and freedom from the grip of resentment. And as I continue on this journey, I do so with a sense of hope and determination, knowing that each step I take brings me closer to a life filled with peace, joy, and forgiveness.

9. **Set Boundaries**: While forgiveness is important, it's also essential to set healthy boundaries to protect yourself from further harm. Establish clear boundaries with the person who hurt you and take steps to safeguard your emotional and physical well-being.

Setting boundaries has become a cornerstone of my journey towards healing and forgiveness. As I've navigated the complexities of forgiveness, I've come to realize the vital importance of establishing clear boundaries to protect myself from further harm and safeguard my emotional and physical well-being. While forgiveness is a noble and necessary endeavor, it does not mean subjecting myself to continued mistreatment or allowing others to disregard my needs and boundaries. Instead, setting boundaries empowers me to assert my worth, prioritize my own well-being, and cultivate healthy, mutually-respectful relationships.

At the outset of my journey, I found the concept of setting boundaries somewhat daunting. It felt like a confrontational and assertive act—a departure from the passive and accommodating stance I had often adopted in the past. However, now, I enjoy setting boundaries, I discovered that it was an act of self-love and self-respect—a way of honoring my own needs and values and affirming my inherent worth as a human being.

One of the most liberating aspects of setting boundaries is the sense of agency and empowerment it brings. By clearly articulating my limits and expectations, I reclaim control over my own life and decisions, rather than allowing others to dictate my boundaries for me. This newfound sense of autonomy allows me to navigate relationships with confidence and assertiveness, knowing that I have the power to protect myself from harm and advocate for my own well-being.

Setting boundaries has enabled me to cultivate healthier and more fulfilling relationships. By clearly communicating my needs and expectations to others, I foster greater understanding and mutual respect within my relationships. Boundaries serve as a roadmap for navigating interpersonal interactions, guiding both myself and others towards behaviors that are respectful, considerate, and conducive to mutual growth and well-being.

But perhaps the most profound aspect of setting boundaries is the sense of relief and liberation it brings. No longer do I feel obligated to tolerate mistreatment or sacrifice my own well-being for the sake of preserving a relationship. Instead, I am free to prioritize my own needs and values, confident in the knowledge that setting boundaries is an act of self-care and self-preservation.

In setting boundaries, I've learned to be firm yet compassionate, assertive yet respectful. It's not about erecting walls or shutting others out, but rather about creating healthy parameters for engagement and interaction. Boundaries allow me to maintain a sense of balance and harmony in my relationships, fostering trust, intimacy, and mutual respect.

Furthermore, setting boundaries has allowed me to establish a greater sense of authenticity and integrity in my relationships. By honoring my own needs and values, I show up more fully and authentically in my interactions with others, fostering deeper connections and more meaningful relationships.

Now I fully understand that setting boundaries has been a transformative and empowering practice on my journey towards forgiveness and healing. It has enabled me to reclaim control over my own life and decisions, cultivate healthier relationships, and prioritize my own well-being. While forgiveness remains a central tenet of my journey, setting boundaries has provided me with the necessary tools and strategies to navigate relationships with confidence, assertiveness, and grace. And as I continue to set boundaries in my life, I do so with a sense of empowerment and liberation, knowing that I am honoring my own worth and fostering relationships that are grounded in respect, understanding, and mutual growth.

10. *Seek Healing*: Finally, seek healing through prayer, meditation, and seeking support from trusted friends, family members, or spiritual advisors. Allow yourself time to grieve and process the pain of the past, knowing that God is with you every step of the way.

Seeking healing has been an essential part of my journey towards forgiveness and reconciliation. It's a process that involves both acknowledging the pain of the past and actively working towards emotional, spiritual, and physical restoration. Through prayer, meditation, and seeking support from trusted friends, family members, and spiritual advisors, I've been able to embark on a journey of healing that has brought me closer to God and to myself.

One of the foundational aspects of seeking healing has been prayer. Through prayer, I've found solace in knowing that God is with me every step of the way—that He sees my pain, hears my cries, and offers comfort and strength in times of need. Prayer has become a lifeline—a way of connecting with the divine and surrendering my burdens at His feet. Whether in moments of quiet reflection or in times of desperation and despair, prayer has provided me with a sense of peace and assurance that I am not alone in my struggles.

Similarly, meditation has been a powerful tool for cultivating inner peace and tranquility amidst the chaos of life. Through the practice of mindfulness meditation, I've learned to quiet the chatter of my mind and be present in the moment, allowing myself to fully experience and process my emotions without judgment or attachment. Meditation has taught me to embrace the present moment with openness and acceptance, allowing me to let go of past hurts and anxieties and find peace in the here and now.

But perhaps one of the most transformative aspects of seeking healing has been seeking support from others. In times of need, I've turned to trusted friends, family members, and spiritual advisors for guidance, encouragement, and empathy. Their presence and support have been a source of strength and comfort, reminding me that I am not alone in my struggles and that there are people who care about my well-being.

Seeking support has allowed me to share my story and experiences with others, fostering a sense of connection and understanding that is essential for healing. By opening up to those who love and care about me, I've been able to release the pent-up emotions and burdens that weigh heavily on my heart, allowing space for healing and renewal to take place.

In seeking healing, I've also learned to give myself permission to grieve—to mourn the loss of what was and to acknowledge the pain and sorrow that accompany forgiveness. Grief is a natural and necessary part of the healing process, allowing us to honor our emotions and experiences and make peace with the past. Through tears and sorrow, I've found strength and resilience, knowing that each step of the grieving process brings me closer to wholeness and healing.

Ultimately, seeking healing is a deeply personal and transformative journey—a journey that requires courage, vulnerability, and a willingness to confront the pain of the past. It's a journey of surrender and release, of forgiveness and reconciliation—a journey that leads us closer to God and to ourselves. And as I continue on this journey, I do so with a sense of gratitude and humility, knowing that healing is not just a destination but a lifelong process of growth, transformation, and renewal.

In my journey of seeking healing, I've encountered moments of both struggle and triumph, moments when the pain of the past felt overwhelming, and moments when the light of hope and healing shone through the darkness. It's been a journey of ups and downs, twists and turns, but through it all, I've remained steadfast in my commitment to finding wholeness and restoration.

One of the challenges I've faced in seeking healing is the temptation to rush the process—to expect instant relief from the pain and suffering that I've endured. In our fast-paced society, we're often conditioned to seek quick fixes and instant gratification, but healing is a journey that unfolds in its own time and at its own pace. It requires patience, perseverance, and a willingness to embrace the discomfort and uncertainty that accompany growth and transformation.

Another challenge I've encountered is the fear of facing my pain head-on—to confront the wounds of the past and relive the traumatic experiences that have shaped me. It's a daunting prospect, one that can evoke feelings of anxiety, sadness, and vulnerability. But I've come to realize that healing begins with acknowledging our pain and allowing ourselves to feel it fully—to grieve for what was lost and to honor the depth of our emotions.

In seeking healing, I've also had to confront my own resistance to vulnerability—to open myself up to the possibility of being hurt again. It's a risk we take whenever we allow ourselves to love and trust others, knowing that there's always the potential for pain and disappointment. But I've learned that true healing requires vulnerability—that we must be willing to let down our guard and allow others to see us as we truly are, scars and all.

Despite these challenges, seeking healing has also been a source of profound joy and transformation in my life. It's been a journey of self-discovery and self-empowerment, as I've learned to reclaim my power and agency in the face of adversity. Through prayer, meditation, and seeking support from others, I've discovered inner reserves of strength and resilience that I never knew I possessed.

Moreover, seeking healing has allowed me to cultivate a deeper connection with God—a God who is intimately acquainted with our pain and suffering and who offers comfort and solace in times of need. Through prayer and spiritual practices, I've felt God's presence guiding me through the darkest valleys and leading me towards the light of healing and restoration.

But perhaps the greatest gift of seeking healing has been the sense of freedom and liberation that comes from letting go of past hurts and embracing forgiveness. It's a weight lifted off my shoulders, a burden lifted from my soul, as I release the grip of bitterness and resentment and embrace a spirit of love and compassion. In forgiveness, I've found the key to unlocking the door to healing—a door that leads to a future filled with hope, joy, and wholeness.

I must say that seeking healing is a journey—a journey of courage, vulnerability, and resilience. It's a journey that requires us to confront our pain and suffering with honesty and compassion, to open ourselves up to the possibility of transformation and renewal. And as I continue on this journey, I do so with a sense of hope and optimism, knowing that healing is not just a distant dream but a tangible reality that awaits us on the other side of our pain.

EMBARKING ON THE PATH of forgiveness has been one of the most challenging yet rewarding journeys of my life. Each of the ten steps to forgiveness has played a crucial role in guiding me along this path, offering me wisdom, strength, and guidance as I navigate the complexities of healing and reconciliation.

First and foremost, prayer has been my anchor—a source of solace and strength in times of doubt and despair. Through prayer, I've found the courage to release feelings of anger and resentment, and to entrust my pain and suffering into God's loving hands. It's a daily practice—a lifeline—that sustains me on this journey, reminding me that I am never alone and that God's grace is always sufficient.

Reflecting on Scripture has also been instrumental in my journey of forgiveness, providing me with timeless wisdom and guidance on the importance of extending grace and compassion to others. The words of Jesus, in particular, serve as a beacon of hope and inspiration, showing me the way towards forgiveness and reconciliation through love and humility.

Acknowledging the hurt has been a necessary step in my healing process, allowing me to confront the pain of the past and acknowledge its impact on my life. It's not easy to face the wounds of the past, but by acknowledging them, I've taken the first step towards healing and transformation.

Releasing resentment has been perhaps one of the most challenging steps on my journey of forgiveness. It's a conscious choice to let go of feelings of bitterness and anger, and to embrace a spirit of forgiveness and compassion instead. But with each act of release, I've felt a weight being lifted off my shoulders, and a sense of freedom and peace filling my heart.

Choosing forgiveness has been a pivotal moment in my journey, a turning point where I've made the decision to extend grace and compassion to those who have wronged me. It's not always easy to forgive, but I've learned that forgiveness is not a sign of weakness, but of strength—a strength that comes from trusting in God's grace and mercy.

Praying for the offender has been a transformative practice, allowing me to cultivate empathy and compassion towards those who have hurt me. It's a humbling reminder that we are all broken and in need of God's love and forgiveness, and that by praying for our offenders, we open ourselves up to the possibility of healing and reconciliation.

Setting boundaries has been essential in protecting myself from further harm and asserting my worth and dignity. It's a way of honoring my own needs and values, and creating a safe and healthy environment for myself to heal and grow.

Seeking healing has been a journey of self-discovery and self-empowerment, as I've learned to confront my pain and embrace the possibility of transformation and renewal. Through prayer, meditation, and seeking support from others, I've found solace and strength in the midst of my struggles, knowing that God is with me every step of the way.

Each of the ten steps to forgiveness has been essential in guiding me along the path of healing and reconciliation. It's a journey that requires courage, humility, and a willingness to trust in God's grace and mercy. But with faith and perseverance, I know that I can achieve forgiveness and find true freedom and peace in my heart.

The journey of forgiveness is not a solitary one—it's a shared experience, one that we undertake together as fellow travelers on the path towards healing and reconciliation. While forgiveness may be challenging at times, I want to offer you encouragement and support as you navigate your own journey. I understand firsthand the struggles and obstacles that you may encounter along the way, but I also know the profound sense of liberation and peace that awaits on the other side.

As we both move forward on this journey of forgiveness, I want to remind you that you are not alone. Together, we can lean on the support of our faith communities, our loved ones, and our spiritual mentors, drawing strength from their wisdom and encouragement. We can also seek solace in the words of Scripture, finding guidance and inspiration in the timeless truths of God's word.

Though the road may be long and arduous, I believe that with prayer and perseverance, we can overcome any obstacle that stands in our way. By practicing the steps of forgiveness daily—praying for our offenders, reflecting on Scripture, setting boundaries, and seeking healing—we can gradually chip away at the walls of resentment and bitterness that have held us captive for so long.

I know that forgiving those who have hurt us deeply is no easy task, but I have faith that with God's help, we can find the strength and courage to extend grace and compassion to those who have wronged us. It may require patience, humility, and a willingness to confront our own pain, but I believe that the rewards of forgiveness far outweigh the challenges we may face along the way.

So let us continue to press forward on this journey of forgiveness, knowing that we do not walk alone. With each step we take, let us lean into the grace and mercy of our loving God, trusting that He is with us always, guiding us towards a future filled with hope, healing, and reconciliation. And though the road may be long and difficult, let us take comfort in the knowledge that we are not defined by our past hurts, but by the boundless love and forgiveness that God offers us each and every day.

HEAVENLY FATHER,

I come before you with a humble heart, seeking your guidance and strength as I embark on the journey of forgiveness. You know the pain and hurt that I carry in my heart, and you see the wounds that have been inflicted upon me by others. Yet, in your infinite wisdom and love, you call me to extend grace and compassion to those who have wronged me, just as you have shown me grace and compassion in my own life.

Lord, I confess that forgiving those who have hurt me deeply is a daunting task—one that I cannot accomplish on my own. But I trust in your promise that with you, all things are possible. Give me the courage to release feelings of anger and resentment, and to embrace a spirit of forgiveness and reconciliation instead. Help me to see my offenders through your eyes, with compassion and empathy, recognizing that they, too, are in need of your love and forgiveness.

Grant me the strength to set healthy boundaries, protecting myself from further harm while still extending grace and compassion to those who have wronged me. Help me to let go of the desire for revenge or retribution, and to instead focus on healing and reconciliation. Fill my heart with your peace, Lord, and help me to trust in your plan for my life, even in the midst of pain and uncertainty.

As I walk this journey of forgiveness, Lord, be my constant companion and guide. Surround me with your love and presence, and grant me the wisdom and discernment to know when and how to extend forgiveness to others. Help me to forgive not just with my words, but with my actions and my heart, so that I may experience true freedom and peace.

Thank you, Lord, for your unfailing love and grace, and for the gift of forgiveness that you offer to each and every one of us. May your love fill my heart and overflow into the lives of those around me, as I strive to live out your commandment to love my neighbor as myself.

In Jesus' name, I pray,

Amen.

BIBLIOGRAPHY

King James Version of the Bible for the scriptures referenced:

- Matthew 6:14-15

- "For if ye forgive men their trespasses, your heavenly Father will also forgive you: But if ye forgive not men their trespasses, neither will your Father forgive your trespasses." (Matthew 6:14-15, KJV)

- Colossians 3:13

- "Forbearing one another, and forgiving one another, if any man have a quarrel against any: even as Christ forgave you, so also do ye." (Colossians 3:13, KJV)

- Job's Prayer for His Friends (Job 42:10-17)

- "And the Lord turned the captivity of Job, when he prayed for his friends: also the Lord gave Job twice as much as he had before." (Job 42:10, KJV)

Meet The Author

Kim Ruff Moore is a multi-talented individual, excelling in various fields including music, writing, public speaking, and entrepreneurship. As a stellar award-winning singer-songwriter, she has captivated audiences with her powerful voice and inspiring lyrics. Her music touches hearts and souls, leaving a lasting impact on all who listen.

In addition to her musical talents, Kim is also an accomplished author, penning books that span a wide range of genres. From children's books that ignite imaginations and teach valuable life lessons to insightful guides on financial matters and relationship advice, Kim's writing resonates with readers of all ages and backgrounds.

As a public speaker, Kim shares her wisdom and experiences with audiences around the world, inspiring and empowering others to pursue their dreams and live life to the fullest. Her engaging speaking style and authentic storytelling make her a sought-after speaker at conferences, workshops, and events.

In the business world, Kim is known for her entrepreneurial spirit and innovative approach to business. She has established herself as a respected businesswoman, with ventures spanning various industries, including publishing, entertainment, and beyond.

With a passion for making a positive difference in the world, Kim continues to pursue her dreams and empower others to do the same. Through her music, writing, speaking engagements, and business ventures, she is leaving a lasting legacy of inspiration, encouragement, and empowerment.